Unlocking
GOD's
Power

GOD WANTS TO HELP YOU and FAITH IS THE KEY

By THOMAS H. WARD

with Historical Biblical Consultant,
Robert W. Miller, Jr.

Matthew 16:19, *"I will give to you the keys of the Kingdom of Heaven"*

Unlocking God's Power

By Thomas H. Ward

With Historical Biblical Consultant, Robert W. Miller, Jr.

Published by:

Transcendent Publishing

PO BOX 66202

ST. PETE BEACH, FL 33736

www.transcendentpublishing.com

ISBN: 978-0-9993125-9-9

Printed in the United States of America.

THE HOLY BIBLE VERSIONS USED IN THIS WORK

The majority of Biblical Scriptures used in this book are taken from *The World English Bible* (WEB). Those are marked with "WEB" and are used as published.

Version Information: "*The World English Bible* (WEB) is a Public Domain (no copyright) Modern English translation of the Holy Bible. That means that you may freely copy it in any form, including electronic and print formats. *The World English Bible* is based on the American Standard Version of the Holy Bible first published in 1901, the Biblia Hebraica Stutgartensa Old Testament, and the Greek Majority Text New Testament. It is in draft form and currently being edited for accuracy and readability."

The King James Version (KJV) is also used to quote Scriptures. These are used as published and are marked accordingly with "KJV" to distinguish which version was used.

Version Information for *The King James Version of the Bible (KJV):* "In 1604, King James I of England authorized that a new translation of the Bible into English be started. It was finished in 1611, just 85 years after the first translation of the New Testament into English appeared (Tyndale, 1526). The Authorized Version, or King James Version, quickly became the standard for English-speaking Protestants. Its flowing language and prose rhythm has had a profound influence on the literature of the past 400 years. The King James Version present on the Bible Gateway matches the 1987 printing. The KJV is public domain in the United States."

CONCERNING THIS BOOK

The content provided in this book has been carefully researched as being the most commonly accepted viewpoints of history within the Christian community. References have been provided for the reader to use if necessary.

It is possible that some of the content may or may not be agreeable with your religious dogma or doctrines of faith. Each reader is free to agree or disagree with the author's statements or the history provided. It is up to each of us to decide what information related to the Bible, God, and our Lord Jesus Christ is desirable and matches our own understanding.

The Holy Bible gives us the Word of God, which was written for us. God's Words tell us many things, but to believe in God and Christ one needs to have faith. The main point of this book is the requirement to have faith. This is stressed throughout the book using various formats.

Hebrews 11:6 (WEB), *Without faith, it is impossible to be well pleasing to him, for he who comes to God must believe that he exists and that he is a rewarder of those who seek him.*

DEDICATION

I would like to dedicate this book to everyone who reads it. May God Bless those that read His Words. **John 1:1 (WEB)**, *In the beginning, was the Word, and the Word was with God, and the Word was God.*

I also dedicate this book to my beloved grandmother Bertha De Breau, the kindest, most gentle person I have ever known. She had real faith in the Lord, so I know God is watching over her. She taught me my first prayer. Thank you, Grandmother.

EXPRESSION OF GRATITUDE

I am grateful to God for giving me the ability to write this book. I have done my best to help spread God's Word. I pray it is good enough in the eyes of the Lord. I am grateful to be a witness for Jesus Christ, our Lord, and Savior.

I am also thankful for the Gideons who help spread the Word of God by placing Bibles in hotel rooms and buildings all around the world. The Gideon Bible helped guide me on my many business trips. May God continue to bless the work of the Gideons.

Finally, I am thankful to my wife for putting up with my long hours of writing and research. Her advice and love helped me to write *Unlocking God's Power*.

ACKNOWLEDGEMENTS

The following people provided their aid, support, and encouragement, which helped me to write *Unlocking God's Power*.

My sincere thanks to Mr. Robert W. Miller, Jr., who is my brother in faith and a close friend. He is a true historian who deals in the facts as written in the Holy Bible. His support, advice, and Biblical research were indispensable and greatly appreciated.

Thank you to Reverend Clem Street. He is a man of God, who provided me encouragement to have this book published.

Thank you to Reverend William Cowfer for his kind support and comments of encouragement. He inspired me to proceed with this book, stating it was possibly a calling from God.

I wish to thank Reverend R. Karnes for his support. He advised me that the task to write about the Bible is not an easy one. He stated, "Maybe you were given inspiration from above to use your skills and help spread the Word of God."

AN INVITATION TO YOU

If you enjoy this book, I invite you to leave a review on Amazon. Your reviews are very important for author ratings and to help spread the message within the book. Thank you.

Email me at ThomasHWardBooks@gmail.com with your comments or suggestions, and receive my next book in PDF for FREE. Only notices about my new books or book giveaways will be sent to you. Your email address will be kept confidential.

Follow me at facebook.com/thomas.ward.71271466.

CONTENTS

PREFACE

In ancient days, did people actually see, hear, and speak to God? What are God's invisible forces? Who really were the twelve disciples? Who were the amazing women disciples? What happened to Mary and Joseph, the parents of Jesus? Why was the village of Capernaum so important? Why did Jesus live there? Who was Joseph of Arimathea? What did he do that was so important for Christianity? Who actually wrote the New Testament? Who were the "Five?" Is there any evidence that Jesus was resurrected? What is the New Covenant? How was the Church actually born? Did Jesus really have brothers and sisters? Where does faith come from?

All these questions and more are answered in *Unlocking God's Power*. Some little-known facts about Jesus, his ministry, and the Old Testament are revealed in this book.

With the blessings of God, this book will take you back in time—back to the beginning of man—and provide you a brief history of the Old Testament. Then it will zoom you through time, covering the life of Jesus Christ and his disciples. *Unlocking God's Power* provides facts and comments about key prophets, Jesus Christ, and the disciples who lived in ancient times that few people know about. New stories and information are provided that will amaze you. You will discover who the ancient people actually were and make a connection with them. It ends with modern-day true stories of miracles and then explains how you can ask God for help.

This is a concise nondenominational history book about the amazing people in the Bible. It's about the people who had faith in God and Jesus and because of this miracles occurred. Read *Unlocking God's Power* and discover a whole new meaning about the Bible and the people who made it all possible. Discover a new message about faith. Find out how to unlock the power of God in your life.

Unlocking God's Power is written for young and old alike to gain a better appreciation of the Bible. Hopefully, you will read it to your children or let them read it to increase their understanding of the Bible. It is written for those who believe in our Heavenly Father and Jesus Christ, and for those who have doubt or don't believe. For those who know nothing about the Bible, it is my hope this book will inspire them to read God's Words more often and accept Christ into their hearts.

One chapter is dedicated to modern-day true stories about miracles, angels, and prayers that have helped people. You can explore how these modern-day stories are related to Bible Scriptures. Maybe you can see yourself in these stories. Maybe you have a story to tell.

There is a chapter covering **Important Subjects** taken from the Bible. God's Words tell us many things that may surprise you. What does the Bible tell us about **ITSELF**, about **GOD**, about **MAN**, about **HEAVEN**, about **SIN**, about **HELL**, about **JESUS CHRIST**, about **FAITH**; and finally, what does the Bible tell us about **LIFE**?

The Bible is the most amazing book ever written. It was written under the divine guidance of God by many people over thousands of years. Generations after generations of people, telling a story about God and Christ. Did all these people just make up these stories because they didn't have anything better to do? No, they were recording the history of the ancient world as God had instructed them to do.

The Bible (from *biblos*, Greek for "book") is the basis of two great religions: Judaism (the Old Testament) and Christianity (the New Testament). It is a collection of ancient documents written with divine guidance to inform us about our Lord God Almighty. The Bible explains the laws and rules of God for his people to follow. It tells what people witnessed and thereby provides a written history of those ancient events.

Pray and God will help you. Reading the Words of God is praying. The Bible Scriptures and prayers in this book have been carefully researched and selected. They are assumed to be the most powerful ones found in the

Bible. Of course, this is a debatable subject since every Scripture and prayer in the Bible is a powerful message from God.

Read *Unlocking God's Power* and discover a whole new meaning to your life. Unlock the meaning of God's Words, and feel God's strength and love. Discover how God works wonders in mysterious ways to improve your life. He is waiting for you. All you have to do is use the key and open the door of faith.

As written in **Matthew 16:19 (KJV)**, Jesus said to Peter, *"And I will give unto thee the keys of the kingdom of heaven: and whatsoever thou shalt bind on earth shall be bound in heaven: and whatsoever thou shalt loose on earth shall be loosed in heaven."*

INTRODUCTION

Reading God's Words, in a sense, is the same as praying. Anytime you are reading God's Words you are communicating with God. You are talking to God and He can hear you.

The following are two of my favorite Bible verses. They are direct and to the point, informing you of God's power and that of Jesus Christ.

Psalm 46:10 (WEB), *"Be still, and know that I am God. I will be exalted among the nations. I will be exalted in the earth."*

John 14:6 (WEB), *Jesus said to him, "I am the way, the truth, and the life. No one comes to the Father, except through me."*

Unlocking God's Power starts with a discussion of God's invisible forces and faith. It seems logical to discuss these invisible forces since God Himself is invisible to us. It stands to reason that the greatest forces in the world would also be invisible to our eyes. We have faith and trust in these forces to help us in our daily lives. What are these invisible forces?

Make no mistake, these forces are provided by God. But, where does faith come from and what does it mean? Continue reading and learn more about faith and God's invisible forces.

Next, this book reviews a few of the most important people in the Old Testament. It provides new insight into Adam and Eve, Cain and Able, Noah, Abraham, Moses, and the great prophets Elijah and Elisha. These people were selected for certain reasons to be mentioned this book. The Old Testament provides us with many answers, but also raises many questions for us to ponder.

Adam and Eve were the first two people on earth, created by God in his image. They were the first people to commit a sin by disobeying God's commandment. The couple was thrown out of the Garden of Eden into the wilderness. What happened to them? What became of the Garden of Eden?

Cain and Able were the first humans to be born on earth, thereby creating the first family. Cain committed the first murder and also sinned. He was given the mark of Cain by God. Cain went to live in the mysterious land of Nod. What was the mark of Cain? Where was the land of Nod? Were there other people living in the land of Nod?

Noah was selected by God to re-populate the earth, with his sons, after the Great Flood. Everyone alive today comes from the seed of Noah. God made the first covenant with Noah. What was that covenant? Why did God select Noah to live? Did only the Noah family survive the flood, or did other people also survive?

Abraham lived one thousand years after Noah. He started the Jewish nation in the land of Canaan, which was promised to him by God. God made a covenant with Abraham. Actually, it was the second covenant made with man. What was that covenant? Why did God choose Abraham? Why did he give Abraham the land of Canaan? What was so special and important about this land?

God, using Moses, set His people free from slavery in Egypt. God helped Moses return the people to the land of Canaan. For the first time, God gave the people miracle tools to help them. God provided the first actual laws for people to follow. What were the miracle tools? Why and how did God's people become slaves in Egypt? What were the new laws provided to them by God? Why was Moses chosen to lead the people? What does Moses have to do with Jesus Christ?

The prophets Elijah and Elisha were faithful servants of God. What did they do that was so important that they are mentioned in the Bible? Who were these special men and where did they come from? How is Elijah connected to Jesus? What amazing miracles did Elisha perform that were similar to the ones Christ accomplished?

After the Old Testament, we jump ahead in time to when the Son of God walked the earth. You may discover new amazing facts about Jesus and his disciples. Christ also had women disciples that few know about. Who were they and what did they do? Who were the people actually responsible for writing the New Testament Scriptures? The original writers may not be whom you think.

Do you know the answers to the above questions?

If not, then please continue reading to learn more about the Bible, faith, and Jesus Christ.

Intertwined with the Scriptures in this book are modern-day true stories of people who have seen a miracle or had one happen to them. These are people who have been in the presence of angels. People who have had prayers answered. People who have witnessed a holy spirit at work firsthand. People who had given up all hope until Christ came into their lives and everything changed for the better.

Read these true contemporary stories, and see how God helped these people in times of need. Read the Scriptures in this book, and see how much they apply to these stories and to your life.

Do you believe in God? Do you believe in Jesus Christ, our Savior? I remember my mother, God bless her soul, taking us to church every Sunday starting at the age of 8. I loved going to Sunday school and learning about God, Jesus, and the Bible. I enjoyed hearing the stories of Jesus and the miracles he performed. Never once did I doubt what I was taught.

However, I didn't fully understand the relationship that God and Jesus had with us at that young age. But it was enlightening and interesting to me. Sunday school sparked a curiosity in me about the Bible and about God Himself. How could there be a God? How could there be a spirit, power, or being that you cannot see or speak to face-to-face? How could Jesus die, come back to life for a short time, and then pass on to heaven? These were questions of a young child.

I was told you must have faith and believe. So, I did believe. I had faith and never doubted the Word of God. I prayed every day, asking God to watch over my family. I said the Lord's Prayer almost every single night. However, many people just do not have faith or believe in God. Many people do not pray at all and have never read the Bible.

I believe man is basically good but is tempted every day by the forces of evil. Some people turn to the dark side without even knowing it. As I became older and had discussions with those who were nonbelievers, I found out why some people don't believe in God. Most were never taught about God and Jesus. They were never exposed to the details of the Bible, and most had never read the Bible. Oh, maybe they read one or two pages, but they had never read or studied the Bible in any depth. They had never used the Bible to help them solve a problem in a time of need. They had never asked God for help by using prayer. They simply didn't know how to pray and would not humble themselves to God and ask for help. These people had never seen a miracle or the power of God at work.

I recall when praying at a young age, I always asked God to watch over my family. I never prayed for a material possession. Then one day, I asked God for something material that my brother and I could use. I said a simple prayer, hoping that my prayer would be answered.

To my wonderment, it was like magic … my prayer was answered. To me, it was a miracle at the age of 10. Some called it luck. But I knew it was God. Within thirty minutes of saying my prayer, it was answered. It shocked me and made me realize the power of God. I never told my father or mother that I prayed to God for something material, because they wouldn't have liked that. I was ashamed after that, for using God's power to obtain something so petty. So, I have never asked God for anything else, unless it was to help others.

In ancient days prophets and certain faithful people were able to talk directly to God or hear him in a dream. There are many stories of the ancients talking to God and seeing some image of God. Prophets and others saw God in human form or in some other form, like a cloud or burning bush. This book discusses some of the most notable encounters between God and man.

A monk named Dionysius Exiguous started the numbering system for the years using the birth of Christ as year one. He used the Latin term anno Domini or "in the year of our Lord" which is why we use the letters AD. This means that we use the birth of Christ to signify something wonderful happened to the world when God's Son came to us. It denotes the beginning of the most amazing time in the history of man. It is the time when people saw the Son of God. It meant that we would all be forgiven for our sins.

Did people actually see Jesus? Was he a real person? Of course, thousands of people saw and spoke to Jesus. Proof of Jesus is provided in this book, which quotes Scriptures as well as ancient texts written about Christ. Many saw him perform miracles of all types. But not only did Jesus perform miracles so did his disciples. Yes, Jesus, through the power of God and the Holy

Spirit, granted his disciples the ability to heal the sick and raise the dead. Even today, people of God, true believers, are able to heal the sick by using prayers to God. Through prayers, people can be healed. They are called unexplainable miracles by most, but people of faith know it was God's hand at work.

As you will see from the stories in this book, God works miracles quickly at times, and at other times slowly. He works in ways that sometimes don't seem to make any sense until later, when you put the whole picture together. Then you realize it was the work of God. By using prayer, you were able to unlock God's power. You spoke to God and He answered you. Was it a miracle? Remember, miracles happen every single day.

THOMAS H. WARD

CHAPTER 1

GOD'S INVISIBLE FORCES
and FAITH

Hebrews 11:3 (WEB), *By faith, we understand that the universe has been framed by the word of God, so that what is seen has not been made out of things which are visible.*

B eing an educated metallurgical engineer, I like to deal with facts and theories that most people don't think about. Engineers deal with the known and unknown, but they always try to find the answers to solve a problem.

As far as I know, modern-day people haven't actually seen God or Christ, but some have seen angels. I have never seen God or heard him directly speak to me. But I know God is real because I have had prayers answered. I have seen miracles with my own eyes, and I know people who have seen angels and spoken to them.

If you believe in God and our Savior Jesus Christ, maybe you have seen a miracle or had a prayer answered. If not, then you haven't unlocked God's power. Maybe you simply don't believe in God and Jesus. Maybe you don't have faith that God and Jesus watch over us.

Consider the following discussion, which uses logic to prove God is real. People who hear strange sounds, see invisible people, smell something different, or do uncommon things aren't all weird or mentally ill. There are strange forces, invisible forces, at play that cannot be explained by anyone. These forces may be good or bad, but their existence cannot necessarily be explained.

The world is made up of many invisible forces. These are forces you can't directly see. All these forces have a positive and negative side to them—or an opposite of each other. This can make them good or bad forces. You say, "Invisible forces, what a bunch of malarkey."

There are probably many that we don't know about, but I can name a few of the known invisible forces. To start with, consider the simplest force, which is the wind. You can't see it or taste it, but you can feel the air blowing ever so invisibly. The wind from a hurricane or tornado can destroy whole cities. It's a very powerful force. The wind in a tornado can be seen indirectly by the dirt and debris swirling around. The wind blowing can be felt or seen by looking at the trees. The wind can also be a good force bringing needed rain or coolness to the desert. The opposite of the wind is no wind, which can also be a positive or negative force of nature. In ancient times no one knew where or how the wind came about. Thanks to modern science we now have some idea as to how the wind is created by God. Continue reading to find out about more unexplainable amazing invisible forces.

Next, consider magnetism. A magnetic field is invisible to your eye, yet the earth's magnetic field can affect anything that is magnetic, like a compass or piece of iron. A magnetic field has a north (positive) and south (negative) pole. One pole attracts and the other repels. There is an invisible magnetic field covering the earth, protecting it from solar winds and radiation from the sun. It is believed that this field is created by the molten metal core in the center of the earth. However, no one really knows how or why it exactly works. No one has ever been to the center of the earth. Most people give no thought to this powerful invisible force here on earth, but it is all around us. It is a mystery we take for granted.

Another great invisible force is electricity. If you touch it and get shocked, you know it's there, but you can't normally see this great invisible force. If it arcs, or shorts, it may cause a spark of light. All of us have seen the power of lightning. For thousands of years, no one knew what it was or how it was created. Like the other invisible forces, electricity has positive and negative sides, which can attract or repel each other. The wonders of electricity are still being discovered. So far, you haven't read about the most amazing invisible forces. The best is yet to come.

There is one more invisible force that affects everyone here on earth. It is the force that influences how you walk or how high you can jump. It is a force that helps to make us safe or it can place us in danger. Maybe you can guess it? What goes up must come down. Right, it's gravity—a force that even today's scientists have a problem explaining.

Gravity is defined in the dictionary as, *"the force of attraction by which terrestrial bodies tend to fall toward the center of the earth."*

Wikipedia says, *"Gravity is most accurately described by the general theory of relativity (proposed by Albert Einstein in 1915) which describes gravity not as a force, but as a consequence of the curvature of space-time caused by the uneven distribution of mass/energy."*

What does that mean? The fact is that even today scientists don't really know what the invisible force of gravity is or exactly where it comes from. They can calculate its effect on objects, but there are only theories as to what really makes gravity. Something that seems so simple cannot be fully explained even by our best NASA scientists. Gravity is truly one of God's great invisible forces.

Years ago, before the electron microscope was invented, atoms, electrons, genes, and DNA all were invisible to our eye. Humans had no idea that these tiny structures of life existed. They had no idea that these were the building blocks of God's life here on earth and in the universe. Refer back to the beginning of this chapter. As stated in **Hebrews**, *"By faith, we understand that the universe has been framed by the word of God,* *so that what is seen has not been made out of things which are visible."*

"What is seen has not been made out of things which are visible." This means that what we see is made or created from invisible things … things we cannot see. This Scripture is the Word of God telling us something that we just discovered in the twentieth century. Everything on earth is made up of atoms which are not visible to us. It's important to carefully read the Scriptures. What other invisible forces are there?

The Van Allen Radiation Belts, discovered in 1958, are totally unexplainable. They are still being studied. The invisible radiation belts were found to be a nearly impenetrable barrier that helps prevent the fastest, highly energetic electrons from reaching the earth. Scientists have learned that the two invisible belts that encircle the earth can change in size, merge, or even separate into three belts. The belts move around changing size and shape as if they are alive, protecting our planet when necessary. Without the belts, we would be bombarded by all types of dangerous space particles, so they are protecting us from potential destruction. It's believed that these belts are related somehow to the earth's magnetic field. They are an invisible force and one of God's greatest mysteries.

There is also a scientific theory that dark matter is a type of matter that makes up 84 percent of the universe. It doesn't absorb light or emit light, so it can't be seen by the human eye. What if there are other so-called invisible forces, objects, things, people, beings, spirits, angels, and—yes—even a God? Is this possible?

Even today with all our knowledge, our best scientists have no idea how some of these invisible forces really work or where they come from. Yes, they have theories that guess at some answers, but they only have theories. Webster's dictionary defines a theory as; *"the analysis of a set of facts in their relation to one another, or abstract thought; speculation, a plausible or scientifically acceptable general principle or body of principles offered to explain phenomena."*

Considering these facts about invisible forces, isn't it possible to open your mind, and most importantly your heart to God and Christ? We now know that Jesus Christ was a real person who walked the earth. The Bible, which is the Word of God, tells us that. Other ancient texts have also confirmed that Jesus lived on this earth. Billions of people confirm this by their faith and belief in the Lord.

Written in the *Annals of Imperial Rome*, around AD 70, by Cornelius Tacitus, one of the greatest Roman historians, is the following: *"Christ suffered the ultimate penalty at the hands of procurator Pontius Pilate when Tiberius was Emperor of Rome."* This one sentence leaves no doubt that Jesus was real and walked the earth.

In the *Antiquities of the Jews*, by a man named Josephus, around AD 37–100, it is written that *"There was a wise man who was called Jesus and his conduct was good. Pilate condemned him to be crucified. His disciples did not abandon their loyalty to him. They reported that he appeared to them three days after his crucifixion and that he was alive."*

The above states that Christ was raised from the dead. People did not take the time to record events in ancient days unless they were believed to be true.

When faced with the concept of God, some people use words like "intelligent designer," "creationism," or some other expression—but never use the word "God." Why don't they use the word "God"? I suggest the main reason is that they cannot see God. They have never spoken to Him and they have never read the Bible. They have never read God's Words and, simply put, they have no faith.

To believe in God one needs to have faith. What does faith mean? Merriam-Webster defines it as: *"(1) belief and trust in and loyalty to God; (2) belief in the traditional doctrines of a religion; (3) firm belief in something for which there is no proof; (4) complete trust."*

Number three above states: *"firm belief in something for which there is no proof."* But the fact is, there is proof. The proof is written in the Bible and in ancient texts. The proof is in the miracles that happen every day.

One just needs to have faith and believe. How does one find faith? Continue reading to find out why others believe and have faith. Perhaps you will find faith, because it is right in front of your own eyes.

Where Does Faith Come From?

Ephesians 2:8 (WEB), *for by grace you have been saved through faith, and that not of yourselves; it is the gift of God, ...*

Matthew 14:28-31 (WEB), *Peter answered him and said, "Lord, if it is you, command me to come to you on the waters."*

He said, "Come!"

Peter stepped down from the boat and walked on the waters to come to Jesus. But when he saw that the wind was strong, he was afraid, and beginning to sink, he cried out, saying, "Lord, save me!"

Immediately Jesus stretched out his hand, took hold of him, and said to him, "You of little faith, why did you doubt?"

Hebrews 11:1 (WEB), *Now faith is assurance of things hoped for, proof of things not seen.*

Comments

It is clear that faith comes from God. It is his gift to us. We are free to accept it or decline it. The choice is up to you. Choose wisely and you may unlock the power of God.

Sometimes, however, God will indirectly speak to you and help you find faith. Just like Jesus helped Peter walk on water, God will guide you to find the faith that you need to do His work. Many people hear God calling. They are blessed with faith to become His disciple or witness. One simply cannot refuse when God summons you. All you have to do is accept His call and believe.

In conclusion, many things on this earth are invisible and unexplainable to us. We have learned to have faith in these invisible forces, which were made by God and will always be there. This is the type of unbroken faith we need to have in God and Christ, who are invisible to our earthly eyes.

Proverbs 3:5-6 (WEB), *Trust in God with all your heart, and don't lean on your own understanding. In all your ways acknowledge him, and he will make your paths straight.*

THOMAS H. WARD

CHAPTER 2

GOD'S LAWS and MORE ABOUT FAITH

J ust look around today at all the turmoil and fighting in various countries around the world. Yes, there have always been wars and turmoil in the ancient past. However, today more countries are in continuous turmoil with mass killing and disarray. With today's modern weapons, killing is easier than it has ever been. There is a lack of law and order in certain countries. Anyone can kill, rob, or rape and get away with it. Many countries have no laws at all or legal system. One can see that most countries in turmoil have little or no belief in the God of our Fathers.

Now consider Western Civilization as it exists today. What do we owe our basic fundamental rights and laws to? The answer is simple: The Ten Commandments given to us by God. These laws did more to make society safer and more humane than any others in history. More than two billion Christians and Jews, as well as non-Christians, know God's Ten Commandments. You might not want to accept this fact if you are a nonbeliever, but most would agree without these laws man would be in greater confusion and turbulence. These laws are the foundation of today's complicated legal system.

The Ten Commandments, written by the finger of God and placed in the Ark of the Covenant, are summarized as follows:

1. You shall have no other gods before Me.

2. You shall make no idols.

3. You shall not take the name of the Lord your God in vain.

4. Keep the Sabbath day holy.

5. Honor your father and your mother.

6. You shall not murder.

7. You shall not commit adultery.

8. You shall not steal.

9. You shall not bear false witness against your neighbor.

10. You shall not covet thy neighbor's wife or anything that belongs to your neighbor.

Refer to **Exodus 20**, **Leviticus 19**, **or Deuteronomy 5** for more complete Scriptures about the Ten Commandments.

Like it or not, the Ten Commandments, written by God on stone tablets, are worldwide laws. They are the building blocks of the civilized world. These laws made the world a better and safer place to live. The Ten Commandments were a blessing given to us so we could make the laws that rule us today.

God also has made other sub-rules for us to obey. The most famous one is the "Golden Rule."

Matthew 7:12 (WEB), *Therefore whatever you desire for men to do to you, you shall also do to them; for this is the law and the prophets.*

The Scriptures contain many such rules and examples to help you live a better life following God's Commandments and the teachings of Jesus Christ.

In society, we follow many rules made by man and by God. The most important rules were created by God, which supersede any rules made by man. We all question man's laws at times, and sometimes we also question some of God's rules that we don't understand.

However, we can be sure that God's rules and laws are made for our benefit. It is God's intention that we, and our society, will have a better chance of survival by following His laws.

The Book of **Proverbs** is very interesting to read because it contains many short writings offering practical advice. What to do and what not to do, to keep favor with the Lord. The following are important examples.

Proverbs 3:5 (WEB), *Trust in the Lord with all your heart, and don't lean on your own understanding.*

Proverbs 6:16-19 (WEB), *There are six things*

which Yahweh hates; yes, seven which are an abomination to him: haughty eyes, a lying tongue, hands that shed innocent blood, a heart that devises wicked schemes, feet that are swift in running to mischief, a false witness who utters lies, and he who sows discord among brothers.

The Book of **Proverbs** was mostly written by Solomon, David's son, who was king of Israel. Solomon reportedly spoke 3,000 proverbs **(1 Kings 4:32)** during his life around 950 BC. Others were written by unidentified men called "The Wise" **(Proverbs 24:23)**. The Solomon proverbs were copied and passed on in writing, as it is stated in **Proverbs 25:1 (WEB)**, *These also are proverbs of Solomon, which the men of Hezekiah king of Judah copied out.*

The Book of **Leviticus** contains many laws and rules that God required the Hebrews to follow. It covers a variety of subjects from how to treat items with mildew or mold to advising what your punishment will be for disobedience. The rules are amazingly complex and very detailed. This book is highly recommended reading to gain a better insight into all the rules and laws that God required the Jews to follow. It is true that many of these rules do not apply today, if you are a Christian, but just the same they are part of God's Words.

So, we can conclude that we know what laws are the most important ones to follow just by looking at the order of the Ten Commandments. We know what God likes and doesn't like. We know that faith is a gift from God. Consider the following verses, which tell us God will answer our prayers if we have faith and believe.

Mark 11:24 (WEB), *Therefore I tell you, "All things whatever you pray and ask for, believe that you have received them, and you shall have them."*

Matthew 21:22 (WEB), *All things, whatever you ask in prayer, believing, you will receive.*

Luke 11:9 (WEB), *I tell you, "Keep asking, and it will be given you. Keep seeking, and you will find. Keep knocking, and it will be opened to you."*

In summary, there are certain things we must do to keep favor in the eyes of the Lord. We need to have faith, trust, devotion, loyalty, and we need to obey God's laws. Always humble yourself and pray, thanking God for your blessings.

It seems pretty easy to do these things. The problem is, it is not so simple because we are always being tempted to commit sins. What else does God expect of us? Please continue reading to find how you can unlock God's power and receive his blessings.

THOMAS H. WARD

CHAPTER 3

THE OLD TESTAMENT

T he standard Old Testament, in the Bible, consists of a total of thirty-nine books. There are, however, other holy documents that have not been published in the Bible for various reasons, which are beyond the scope of this book.

The Old Testament starts at the beginning of time as we know it. It is the beginning of the universe and the earth, which were created by God Almighty. It is the written history recorded thousands of years ago by people who believed in God. It was recorded by ancient people who spoke to God and/or saw the Lord. Many stories were passed down verbally until writing was invented. Then a tangible permanent history was made inspired and guided by the Lord.

Did Ancient Biblical People Actually See God?

Let us ponder and consider the fact that we cannot see God. In ancient times the Bible tells us that selected people did see God in different forms. In those days some people were able to speak directly to God and hear his reply. How do we know this? The Bible tells us the names of people who spoke to God.

Of course, doubters always ask: "Did this really happen? There is no proof." Well, the good news is, there is proof. Ancient texts confirm many of the stories in the Old and New Testament. Do you think people just sat around and made up these incredible stories? Did they just dream them up off the top of their heads for thousands of years about the same God? Did generation after generation of people make up stories about God? Why would they do that if God wasn't real, and to what end?

People didn't have the time to sit around and dream up stories, as they were too busy trying to stay alive two thousand to ten thousand years ago. In the ancient days, people needed to hunt and farm every day just to stay alive. They had busy lives tilling the fields and tending the sheep, working from daybreak until dark every day. Besides, most people didn't know how to read or write. If they wanted to record an event, they would have to pay a scribe to do so. No, they didn't dream up these stories, because in those days you would be considered strange and most likely banned from the village or put to death for being evil.

It can be concluded that if someone saw an image of God, spoke to him or an angel, it was deemed so important that people took the time to make a record of that event. Only important real events were recorded. They had no time for telling and recording tall tales. It was a different world in ancient times, and writing anything down was a very serious matter of recording history.

Did people actually see God? If you believe the Bible, yes, they did, but most likely what these people saw was a representation of God and not God's actual living spirit. God as a spirit is invisible to humans. No one can see him directly. To see God in his original form means death to the beholder.

Consider the following Scripture verses about seeing God. These verses state that no man may see the true God and live.

1 Timothy 6:16 (WEB), *who alone has immortality, dwelling in unapproachable light; whom no man has seen, nor can see: to whom be honor and eternal power. Amen.*

Exodus 33:18-20 (WEB), *Moses said, "Please show me your glory."*

God said, "I will make all my goodness pass before you, and will proclaim Yahweh's name before you. I will be gracious to whom I will be gracious, and will show mercy to whom I will show mercy."

And God said, "You cannot see my face, for man may not see me and live."

John 1:18 (WEB), *No one has seen God at any time. The one and only Son, who is in the bosom of the Father, he has declared Him.*

The next chapter reviews a few of the people who had some type of contact with God based on the Old Testament. They are; Adam and Eve, Cain and Able, Noah, Abraham, Moses, Elijah, and Elisha. Read the stories about them and find out why they did what God asked them to do. Why did they have such faith in God? Put yourself in their place. Would you do the same as they did? Would you follow the commands of God? Do you have enough faith to trust the Lord God?

CHAPTER 4

OLD TESTAMENT PEOPLE WHO
SAW and/or SPOKE TO GOD

The following is a synopsis of three books in the Old Testament (Genesis, Exodus, and Kings). Now let us examine just a few of the people in ancient days who spoke to God and/or saw an image of him. God has been seen in many forms in the Bible. He has been seen as a normal person, as a cloud of glory, as a burning bush, and one of my favorites, riding on a chariot of fire pulled by horses on fire. There are many passages of Scripture that indicate people actually saw an image of God, or at least spoke to him. These are people who carried on actual conversations with the Lord. The following are a few of the most notable conversations and interactions between God and man in the beginning.

You may know the following Scriptures very well but read them again. Try to read between the lines to imagine how these people felt and thought. Think about the faith that these ancient people must have had in God Almighty to do what they did. Their faith, for the most part, was unquestionable.

THE BOOK OF GENESIS

Genesis is the beginning of man. It also is the beginning of time as we know it. No one knows when the beginning of time actually started for man. It could have been ten thousand years ago or even two hundred thousand years ago. The Book of Genesis covers an immense amount of time. Man was formed in God's image; the Bible tells us. It all starts with Adam and Eve, who some believe were the first sinners on earth.

Adam and Eve

The very first two-way conversation God has with man, that is written in the Bible is with Adam and Eve. This is the beginning of the human race. Adam and Eve had eaten of the forbidden fruit of knowledge. God is not happy about that.

Genesis 3:9-13 (WEB), *Yahweh called to the man, and said to him, "Where are you?"*

The man said, "I heard your voice in the garden, and I was afraid because I was naked, and I hid myself."

God said, "Who told you that you were naked? Have you eaten from the tree that I commanded you not to eat from?"

The man said, "The woman whom you gave to be with me, she gave me fruit from the tree, and I ate it."

God said to the woman, "What have you done?"

The woman said, "The serpent deceived me, and I ate."

God didn't like this and commented that he would remove man from the garden of Eden.

Genesis 3:22-24 (WEB), *Yahweh said, "Behold, the man has become like one of us, knowing good and evil. Now, lest he reach out his hand, and also take of the tree of life, and eat, and live forever..." Therefore, God sent him out from the garden of Eden, to till the ground from which he was taken. So, he drove out the man; and he placed cherubim at the east of the garden of Eden, and a flaming sword which turned every way, to guard the way to the tree of life.*

Comments

It is interesting to note that in Genesis it doesn't mention that Adam or Eve actually saw God. Put yourself in the place of Adam and Eve. You are in the Garden of Eden having a great time. You have no worries and no cares.

Then you eat from the Tree of Knowledge, even though your creator, or Father, had told you not to. You didn't stop to think what you were doing because you could not reason so well. But then, you eat of the tree and all of sudden you are able to think and reason between good and evil. You discover you are naked, and now you know you have done wrong.

As God throws you out of the garden, never to return, you are terrified. You wonder what will happen to you. How will you obtain food and shelter? Will we die, like God told us since we ate of the Tree of Knowledge?

GENESIS 2:17 (KJV), *"But of the tree of the knowledge of good and evil, thou shalt not eat of it: for in the day that thou eatest thereof thou shalt surely die"*

But you have eaten from the forbidden tree, and suddenly you are able to think and reason. Still, however, you are afraid, for you know nothing about the world outside of Eden. You have no idea what is beyond the gates of paradise, so you must trust in God for help.

Now, God did not trust Adam and feared he would eat from the Tree of Life and live forever like God. So, God stations cherubim to guard the entrance to Eden with a flaming sword. A cherub is an attendant to the Lord and a protector of anything holy per God's instructions.

God did not let Adam and Eve die, but punished them for eating from the tree. God showed mercy and continued to look after them even outside of the Garden of Eden. They were blessed with two children, Cain and Able.

What does Eden mean? In Hebrew, the meaning is similar to "paradise." In Aramaic, it means "fruitful and well-watered." Where was the Garden of Eden? The Bible tells us in **Genesis 2**, that the garden was in the east, in Eden. Where is Eden? No one knows exactly, but clues tell us in the Bible that a river flowed into the garden and from there it separated into four headwaters or rivers. They were named the Pishon, which wound through the land of Havilah, the Gihon River that ran

4 | OLD TESTAMENT: PEOPLE WHO SAW AND/OR SPOKE TO GOD

through the land of Cush, the Tigris that ran along the east side of Asshur, and the Euphrates River.

Of these rivers, the Tigris and Euphrates are the only two rivers shown on a modern map. It is not known where the lands of Havilah, Cush, and Asshur were located. So, it is not clear where the garden was exactly located.

It seems that the Garden of Eden was a special place for God because he was walking around in the cool of the day. It contained the Tree of Life and the Tree of Knowledge. That sounds like it was God's garden or a place where he dwelled here on earth. As special as it was the Garden of Eden just disappears from Bible Scripture. What happened to it?

The only conclusion that can be reached is that the Garden of Eden was destroyed during the Great Flood. Everything about the landscape would have been altered. Mountains and rivers were changed and valleys were made where none were before. Thus, we are left wondering about the location of Eden.

Cain and Abel

Cain and Abel, sons of Adam, are the first two people born on earth, by Eve. Abel is a shepherd and Cain a farmer. They both made offerings to God. But it seems that for some reason God looked on Abel's offering with more favor, which made Cain jealous. Cain took action.

Genesis 4:6-15 (WEB), *Yahweh said to Cain, "Why are you angry? Why has the expression on your* *face fallen? If you do well, won't it be lifted up? If you don't do well, sin crouches at the door. Its desire is for you, but you are to rule over it."*

Cain said to Abel, his brother, "Let's go into the field." While they were in the field, Cain rose up against Abel, his brother, and killed him.

Yahweh said to Cain, "Where is Abel, your brother?"

He said, "I don't know. Am I my brother's keeper?"

Yahweh said, "What have you done? The voice of your brother's blood cries to me from the ground. Now you are cursed because of the ground, which has opened its mouth to receive your brother's blood from your hand. From now on, when you till the ground, it won't yield its strength to you. You will be a fugitive and a wanderer on the earth."

Cain said to Yahweh, "My punishment is greater than I can bear. Behold, you have driven me out today from the surface of the ground. I will be hidden from your face, and I will be a fugitive and a wanderer on the earth. Whoever finds me will kill me."

Yahweh said to him, "Therefore whoever slays Cain, vengeance will be taken on him sevenfold." Yahweh appointed a sign for Cain, so that anyone finding him would not strike him.

So, God put a mark on Cain and he left God's sight to live in the land of Nod which was east of Eden. Suddenly, Cain has a wife who gave birth to a son named Enoch. They begin to multiply in number.

Genesis 4:17-18 (WEB), *Cain knew his wife. She conceived and gave birth to Enoch. He built a city, and called the name of the city, after the name of his son, Enoch. To Enoch was born Irad. Irad became the father of Mehujael. Mehujael became the father of Methushael. Methushael became the father of Lamech.*

Adam and Eve have another child, a boy named Seth, as noted in **Genesis 4: 25-26 WEB)**, *Adam knew his wife again. She gave birth to a son, and named him Seth, saying, "For God has given me another child instead of Abel, for Cain killed him." A son was also born to Seth, and he named him Enosh. At that time men began to call on Yahweh's name.*

From this time on men begin to call on God. The Scripture follows the family line of Adam, from Seth to Noah. From this point on Cain and his family are not mentioned anymore.

Comments

This was the first murder. The very first cold-blooded murder committed on earth. One cannot help but wonder why God didn't somehow prevent this from happening. God had a reason for this, and many have speculated as to why, but no one knows for sure. What do you think was God's reason? One also wonders what was wrong with Cain. How could he do such a thing and kill his only brother? Why wasn't Cain afraid of what might happen to him? Did he know he was committing a sin?

Maybe not. Maybe this is why God let him live, but in shame with the mark of Cain. What is the mark of Cain?

The mark of Cain was to help keep him from being harmed by others. It didn't guarantee that he wouldn't be killed. The mark only meant a worse fate was in store for anyone who harmed him. We cannot be certain whether the mark was an actual physical sign on his body or something else. The Bible doesn't explain what the mark is.

The Bible says that Cain went to live in the land of Nod. Nod is a mysterious place, and no one knows where it was located, even today. In Hebrew, Nod means "wanderer or exile." The big question is, who was living in the land of Nod? Since Cain, Abel, Adam, and Eve were the only people on earth at the time, it makes you wonder. Some speculate that Cain's wife was a sister or granddaughter of Adam and Eve. This, however, is not mentioned in the Bible. Would Adam let Cain take a sister of the brother he killed?

So, who was living in the land of Nod? Maybe the Adam and Eve family were not the only beings on earth. The Bible clearly indicates that Cain found a wife in the land of Nod and had children. How is that possible?

This leaves us to speculate that Cain's wife was somehow a related to him or God had created some other type of human that the Bible doesn't discuss. After all, God doesn't need to tell us everything he does or why. Remember, the Old Testament is a story about God's chosen people, the Hebrews, and not about other people who may have been on earth at the time. It does raise a few questions for us to ponder.

This is why we need to pay attention to what the Bible tells us and what it doesn't tell us. Keeping your faith when there are unanswered questions is very important. We don't know all the answers to the questions raised in the Bible.

Noah

The Bible states that Noah walked with God. However, in the Bible, there is no actual written two-way dialogue recorded between Noah and God. God gives Noah orders, and he follows God's direction without question.

As we move forward in time from Adam to Noah, ten generations have gone by. It seems the descendants of the Adam and Eve family were not living up to God's expectations. God wasn't pleased with man and the Sons of God for the sins they were committing. God decided to wipe the earth clean and start all over. He spared one good righteous man, Noah, and his family, along with some animals to restart the earth after the great flood.

Genesis 6:3 (WEB), *Yahweh said, "My Spirit will not strive with man forever, because he also is flesh; so, his days will be one hundred twenty years."*

Genesis 6:7 (WEB), *Yahweh said, "I will destroy man whom I have created from the surface of the ground—man, along with animals, creeping things, and birds of the sky—for I am sorry that I have made them."*

After the flood man was starting all over again.

Noah was, in a sense, the new Adam. His sons and their wives would have to repopulate the earth. Up until the flood, men lived well over eight hundred years. God changed that, and after the flood, the lifespan of man was slowly reduced. God's target was a lifespan of one hundred twenty years.

Genesis 9:18-19 (WEB), *The sons of Noah who went out from the ship were Shem, Ham, and Japheth. Ham is the father of Canaan. These three were the sons of Noah, and from these, the whole earth was populated.*

Comments

What most people don't realize is that we all descended from Noah and his three sons, who were Shem, Ham, and Japheth. After the flood, they were the only people alive, according to the Bible. But were they really the only ones left alive? We know God wanted to purge the earth and wipe it clean of man. Is it possible some others survived? Are the other survivors not mentioned because they didn't believe in the one true God? Or did the ancient Hebrews just leave those people out of the writings, since they were not concerned with them and they were not part of God's story? The following in **Genesis** raises the question.

The Bible states in **Genesis 6:4 (KJV)**, *There were giants in the earth in those days; and also after that, when the sons of God came in unto the daughters of men, and they bare children to them, the same became mighty men which were of old, men of renown.*

This states that giants, also known as "Nephilim," were on the earth in those days and also after that. Does this mean before and after the flood? It seems so. It seems they apparently survived the flood. Who were these giant people? Over two thousand years later, in a famous fight, David kills the giant Goliath, who is assumed to have been one of the Nephilim.

How is this possible? We simply don't know. There are many theories about the Nephilim, who they were and where they came from. The theories and speculations about them are beyond the scope of this book.

Did other people live through the flood? We simply don't know that either since the Old Testament was written by the Hebrews. Putting it another way, they wrote the Words of God that they were inspired write, with God's blessings. Some of those other cultures may have believed in and worshiped Almighty God, but we just don't know all the facts. God may have spared other believers that we don't know about.

We don't know what God was thinking or doing. After all, who are we to question God? God doesn't have to tell us everything he is doing or why he does it. Once again, we must have faith and trust in the Lord.

The Bible tells us many people lived over 800 years. We do know that after the flood, the lifespan of man was greatly reduced over the next one thousand years. Noah lived to be 950 years old. No one in the future would live this long again.

It is clear that Noah and his family had great faith

in God. Because of this, they became our forefathers.

Abraham (Abram)

After the Great Flood man starts over with God's help. From Noah to Abram covers a time span of over one thousand years. The line of patriarchs is as follows: Shem, Arphazad, Salah, Eber, Peleg, Reu, Serug, Nahor, Nimrod, Terah, and Abraham.

Generations after the flood, Abraham was born. Abraham's father, Terah, took his family from the city of Ur, located in modern-day Iraq, and decided to move to Canaan for some unknown reason. But he stopped in the city of Haran along the way. There he died at the age of 205 years old.

Genesis 11:27-32 (WEB), *Now these are the generations of Terah: Terah begat Abram, Nahor, and Haran; and Haran begat Lot.*

And Haran died before his father Terah in the land of his nativity, in Ur of the Chaldees.

And Abram and Nahor took wives: the name of Abram's wife was Sarai; and the name of Nahor's wife, Milcah, the daughter of Haran, the father of Milcah, and the father of Iscah.

But Sarai was barren; she had no child.

And Terah took Abram his son, and Lot the son of Haran his son's son, and Sarai his daughter in law, his son Abram's wife; and they went forth with them from Ur of the Chaldees, to go into the land of Canaan; and they came unto Haran, and dwelt there.

And the days of Terah were two hundred and five years: and Terah died in Haran.

What isn't exactly stated in the Bible is that Terah was a man of God. This information was found written in ancient cuneiform clay tablets discovered in the lost city of Ur. He was a holy man of some type and most likely it was God who directed him to move to Canaan.

God made Abraham an offer he could not refuse. God wanted Abraham to move to Canaan and promised him the land of milk and honey. He promised that Abraham would prosper and multiply. But why did God want him to move Canaan?

Genesis 12:7 (WEB), *Yahweh appeared to Abram and said, "I will give this land to your offspring." He built an altar there to Yahweh, who had appeared to him.*

For reasons not exactly known to us, God really loved Abraham. He became God's chosen one and God told him in **Genesis 15:1 (WEB)**, *After these things Yahweh's word came to Abram in a vision, saying, "Don't be afraid, Abram. I am your shield, your exceedingly great reward."*

Maybe it was because he was faithful, humble, and honest and that's why God chose him. There are many two-way conversations between God and Abraham recorded in the Bible.

Abraham's family left Haran and made it to Canaan all right. The time period is around 2091 BC. There they traveled and worked the land of Canaan making it their own. Then a great famine came to the land of Canaan, so the tribe went to Egypt where they knew there would be crops and grass for their animals. The Bible says they lived there for a while giving no idea as to the length of time.

In Egypt, Abraham became wealthy thanks to the Pharaoh's generosity and God's plan. It seems that the Egyptians and the Hebrews became friends. The Pharaoh had eyes for Sarah, Abram's wife as told in **Genesis 12:10-20**. After God saved Sarah from the Pharaoh they returned to Canaan to reclaim their land.

God changed Abram's name to Abraham, meaning father of many, when he was ninety-nine years old. This is when the practice of circumcision started. God required all men, related in any way to Abraham, to be circumcised as a sign of the covenant between Abraham and God.

Genesis 17:1-2 (WEB), *When Abram was ninety-nine years old, Yahweh appeared to Abram, and said to him, "I am God Almighty. Walk before me, and be blameless. I will make my covenant between me and you, and will multiply you exceedingly."*

Genesis 17:5 (WEB), *Your name will no more be called Abram, but your name will be Abraham; for I have made you the father of a multitude of nations.*

Genesis 17:11 (WEB), *You shall be circumcised in the flesh of your foreskin. It will be a token of the covenant between me and you. He who is eight days old will be circumcised among you, every male throughout* *your generations, he who is born in the house, or bought with money from any foreigner who is not of your offspring.*

One day, God suddenly appears to Abraham in human form along with two human angels. Abraham knows who they are without even asking. God is going to investigate the cities of Sodom and Gomorrah who have been committing sins. Abraham makes an emotional plea to God not to destroy the cities and kill everyone.

Genesis 18:20-33 (WEB), *Yahweh said, "Because the cry of Sodom and Gomorrah is great, and because their sin is very grievous, I will go down now, and see whether their deeds are as bad as the reports which have come to me. If not, I will know."*

The men turned from there and went toward Sodom, but Abraham stood yet before Yahweh. Abraham came near, and said, "Will you consume the righteous with the wicked? What if there are fifty righteous within the city? Will you consume and not spare the place for the fifty righteous who are in it? Be it far from you to do things like that, to kill the righteous with the wicked, so that the righteous should be like the wicked. May that be far from you. Shouldn't the Judge of all the earth do right?"

Yahweh said, "If I find in Sodom fifty righteous within the city, then I will spare the whole place for their sake."

Abraham answered, "See now, I have taken it on myself to speak to the Lord, although I am dust and ashes. What if there will lack five of the fifty righteous? Will you destroy all the city for lack of five?"

He said, "I will not destroy it, if I find forty-five there."

He spoke to him yet again, and said, "What if there are forty found there?"

God said, "I will not do it for the forty's sake."

He said, "Oh don't let the Lord be angry, and I will speak. What if there are thirty found there?"

God said, "I will not do it if I find thirty there."

He said, "See now, I have taken it on myself to speak to the Lord. What if there are twenty found there?"

God said, "I will not destroy it for the twenty's sake."

He said, "Oh don't let the Lord be angry, and I will speak just once more. What if ten are found there?"

God said, "I will not destroy it for the ten's sake."

Yahweh went his way, as soon as he had finished communing with Abraham, and Abraham returned to his place.

Later God decides to test Abraham, as stated in **Genesis 22:1-2 (WEB)**, *After these things, God tested Abraham, and said to him, "Abraham!"*

He said, "Here I am."

God said, "Now take your son, your only son Isaac,

whom you love, and go into the land of Moriah. Offer him there as a burnt offering on one of the mountains which I will tell you of."

Abraham did as God ordered him to do. He was about to kill his son Isaac when he heard a voice. An angel of the Lord stopped Abraham just before he put the knife to Isaac's throat. God blessed him, *"Your descendants will take possession of the cities of their enemies and through your offspring all nations on earth will be blessed, because you have obeyed me."* (**Genesis 22:17-18**)

Abraham passed away at the age of 175, leaving everything to his son Isaac.

Genesis 25:7-11 (WEB), *These are the days of the years of Abraham's life which he lived: one hundred seventy-five years. Abraham gave up his spirit, and died in a good old age, an old man, and full of years, and was gathered to his people. Isaac and Ishmael, his sons, buried him in the cave of Machpelah, in the field of Ephron, the son of Zohar the Hittite, which is before Mamre, the field which Abraham purchased from the children of Heth. Abraham was buried there with Sarah, his wife. After the death of Abraham, God blessed Isaac, his son. Isaac lived by Beer Lahai Roi.*

Beer Lahai Roi means a fountain of water in the wilderness. It was near the cities of Kadesh and Bered in ancient days.

Comments

Abraham finished his life in Canaan leaving all to his son Isaac who married Rebecca, the daughter of Bethuel, who was the son of Nahor, the brother of Abraham. He was buried next to his first wife Sarah, in a cave he had purchased years before. Abraham was the founder of the Jewish nation.

In Genesis God appears many times to Abraham, but it seems his form is usually that of a man. Three strangers appear at Abraham's tent. Two are angels and one of them is God. Abraham sees God as a man, but knows it is God right away without being told so.

Abraham talks face-to-face with God pleading for the lives of the people living in Sodom and Gomorrah. It is a moving conversation between Abraham and God. The conversation shows how forgiving and flexible God can be.

One wonders why Abraham pled for the lives in Sodom? Was it because his nephew Lot was living there? The story ends with the angels of God saving Lot, his wife, and two daughters by sending them to the city of Zoar to be safe. Lot's wife dies anyway, turning into a pillar of salt, because she turned to view the city after she was warned not to do so by the angel of God. Then Sodom and Gomorrah were wiped from the face of the earth never to be found again, until 2015.

Many doubted that these cities were real, but in 2015 the actual cities were discovered by archeologists, including the city of Zoar. Proving the Bible was correct again. The cities had been destroyed by some type of unexplainable force. Zoar, on the other hand, was still recognizable as a city even after being buried by the sands of time for thousands of years.

It is clear that Abraham had amazing faith in God, and followed his commands to the letter. Abraham almost killed his only son as per God's instructions. Truly Abraham was a man that God could trust.

Years later, long after Abraham's death, the promised land had another terrible famine, which forced the Hebrews once again to flee to Egypt in search of food. Now Jacob had become the leader of the Hebrews.

It was God's plan that one in the family, named Joseph, would be waiting for them in Egypt. Joseph, with the help of God, had become a powerful ruler in Egypt.

THE BOOK EXODUS

Exodus is an amazing story of the interaction between God, Moses, and the people. Moses speaks to God many times and sees God in different forms. It denotes a new beginning in the relationship between God and the Hebrews because new laws are provided for the people to follow. These laws would test their faith and loyalty to God.

The following is a summary of Exodus the second book of the Bible and the story of Moses. Exodus, a book written by Moses, is the story of God freeing his chosen people from slavery and creating a nation with laws to help govern the people. Moses is the man selected by God to help make all this happen. The great Exodus takes place about 1,400 BC and involved an estimated six hundred thousand Hebrew people.

Skipping forward through time from Abraham to Moses the line of patriarchs looks like this: Abraham, Ishmael, Isaac, Jacob, Joseph, and Moses. Isaac, the son of Abraham, had passed on and now Jacob was the leader.

First, let us backtrack to Genesis where it is noted that Jacob, with the aid of his son Joseph, brought the Hebrews to Egypt to escape another terrible famine in Canaan, with God's blessings. While in Egypt Jacob dies leaving Joseph in charge. It seems the Hebrews go to Egypt whenever there is a famine. This is the second time this has happened in the Old Testament. Egypt at the time was better off than most countries because of the Nile River, known as the "River of Life." Crops could grow almost all year long because of the excellent water supply.

The Hebrews were welcomed with open arms into Egypt because, Joseph, the son of Jacob, was second in command under the king of Egypt. How this all came to be can be found in **Genesis 41 – 50**. It is the story of how Joseph came to be in Egypt at the right time to help the Hebrews, God's chosen people.

The Hebrews were very well off in Egypt when Joseph was alive. However, they stayed far too long in Egypt (over four hundred years) and were turned into slaves by new pharaohs long after Joseph died, at the age of 110. His body was placed in a coffin and buried in Egypt. Now the Hebrews were left without a leader. Later, when the exodus occurred, Moses took the bones of Joseph with him out of Egypt.

The Hebrews now suffered greatly under the bonds of their Egyptian taskmasters. They were so numerous that the pharaoh feared them, so he ordered that every newborn boy must be killed to control the population.

Moses

The story starts here as Moses is raised in an Egyptian royal household. The woman who found baby Moses floating in a basket on the Nile River was a princess and she adopted him. She wasn't just any princess because her father was the Pharaoh of Egypt.

Moses is one of the most famous people in history. He is also one of the most interesting people who had many two-way conversations with God. He actually saw God in many different forms.

Moses was the right man for the job. He was a man who could organize and write in different languages because of his Egyptian education. He was a great manager and leader, and that's why God selected him to help free His people. Moses freed the Hebrews from slavery in Egypt, under God's direction and guidance.

Moses was born to Amram and Jochebed, who were from the tribe of Levite. They were work slaves in Egypt. Moses had one brother, Aaron, who three years older, and also an older sister, Miriam.

Jochebed put baby Moses in a basket and floated him away on the Nile River to save his life from the king's guards. She was praying he would be spared by God and be given a good home. God made sure he found one of the best. The king of Egypt's daughter found him, and Moses was raised as a royal prince. The princess named him Moses meaning, "I drew him out of the water."

After Moses had grown older he discovered that he was really the son of slaves. It must have been a shock to him because he saw how the people suffered under slavery. One day as Moses made his rounds among the people, he saw a guard beating a Hebrew slave half to death and became angry. Either by accident or on purpose Moses killed the guard. The story assumes he feared for his life and status, so he fled Egypt to be a free man and have a simple life. He most likely was confused knowing he was a son of Hebrew slaves, but also because he was raised as an Egyptian Prince. It had to be a depressing situation going from a prince to a desert nomad.

While living in the wilderness (the land of Midian) he married the daughter of a sheepherder, who was a local man of God. His father-in-law's name was Jethro and he was the priest of Midian. So, Moses probably learned something about God from his father-in-law, Jethro. He lived there for another forty years.

He was tending sheep one day at the base of Mount Horeb (the mountain of God) and spotted a burning bush. The bush was on fire but the leaves were not being burned or consumed. He goes closer to examine the unusual sight, amazed by what he is seeing. As he approaches the flaming bush, Moses hears his name being called.

The first two-way conversation between Moses and God starts here. Moses hears God calling his name and falls to his knees in shock, afraid to look at the burning bush.

God then proceeds to tell Moses his plan to free the Hebrew slaves, using Moses. God commanded Moses to return to Egypt and help free his people. At first, Moses didn't think it was a good idea for God to use him, but the Lord changed his mind. Moses comes from the tribe of Levites whom God will make the future priests. They will help spread God's laws among the people.

Exodus 3:1-6 (WEB), *Now Moses was keeping the flock of Jethro, his father-in-law, the priest of Midian, and he led the flock to the back of the wilderness, and came to God's mountain, to Horeb. Yahweh's angel appeared to him in a flame of fire out of the middle of a bush. He looked, and behold, the bush burned with fire, and the bush was not consumed. Moses said, "I will turn aside now, and see this great sight, why the bush is not burnt."*

When Yahweh saw that he turned aside to see, God called to him out of the middle of the bush, and said, "Moses! Moses!"

He said, "Here I am."

God said, "Don't come close. Take your sandals off

of your feet, for the place you are standing on is holy ground." Moreover, he said, "I am the God of your father, the God of Abraham, the God of Isaac, and the God of Jacob."

Moses hid his face; for he was afraid to look at God.

Exodus 33:18-20 (WEB), *Moses said, "Please show me your glory."*

God said, "I will make all my goodness pass before you, and will proclaim Yahweh's name before you. I will be gracious to whom I will be gracious, and will show mercy on whom I will show mercy."

God said, "You cannot see my face, for man may not see me and live."

After using miracles from God, the Hebrews were freed from Egypt. God started to return them to the land of Canaan, which was the Promised Land, but along the way, they stopped at Mount Sinai to pay respects to the Lord.

At Mount Sinai, God told Moses the following: **Exodus 19: 5-6 (KJV)**, *"Now therefore, if ye will obey my voice indeed, and keep my covenant, then ye shall be a peculiar treasure unto me above all people: for all the earth is mine:*

And ye shall be unto me a kingdom of priests, and an holy nation. These are the words which thou shalt speak unto the children of Israel."

It is here that God provides them with the Ten

Commandments and the Ark of Testimony, also known as the Ark of the Covenant. This was the time that God established many new laws for the Hebrews to follow.

Comments

God's name, "I am," is actually pronounced as "Yahweh" (YHWH) in Hebrew. God tells us his name in **Isaiah 42:8 (KJV)**, *"I am the LORD; that is, my name! I will not give my glory to another or my praise to idols."* In some Bibles LORD is replaced with JEHOVAH.

Moses saw the burning bush, but not even Moses ever saw the real face of God. Later, Moses and his people would see God as a cloud in the daytime and a cloud of fire at night. The Cloud of God would lead them to the Promised Land.

What is unique about the Book of Exodus, is that this is the first time God has given the people a **physical article** of any kind. The Ten Commandments were written by the finger of God. It was not written on sheepskin or on any type of paper, but on stone so it would last forever. God also provided Moses with other laws and rules to follow. Moses wrote them all down in the Book of Laws, also called the Book of Moses.

God gave a miracle staff to Moses and Aaron to use so they could confront the pharaoh and free their people. They called it the Staff of God. It parted the Red Sea, brought forth water from rocks in the desert, and provided the ten plagues to the Egyptians that freed the people.

God designed and helped the Israelites build the Ark of the Covenant. The stone tablets were to be kept in the Ark. The Ark was an incredible communication device that permitted the people to talk to God through the priests. It was also a weapon for the Israelites to use with God's permission when he deemed it proper. Where the Ark went, so did God. The Ark of God became the most important item that the Hebrews possessed.

So, this is the first time in the Bible that God gave **miracle tools** to the people. Tools that would prove He was the one and only true God. With these tools many different miracles where performed.

The Hebrews finally return to the Promised Land of milk and honey, but Moses never enters it. He never crosses the Jordan River into the new land. He climbs Mount Nebo for a last look at Canaan, the Promised Land. Shortly thereafter, Moses dies at the age of 120, passing the leadership to Joshua. God had commissioned Joshua, as stated in **Deuteronomy 31**, to be the new leader of the people.

Deuteronomy 34:1-7 (KJV), *And Moses went up from the plains of Moab unto the mountain of Nebo, to the top of Pisgah, that is over against Jericho. And the Lord shewed him all the land of Gilead, unto Dan, And all Naphtali, and the land of Ephraim, and Manasseh, and all the land of Judah, unto the utmost sea, And the south, and the plain of the valley of Jericho, the city of palm trees, unto Zoar.*

And the Lord said unto him, This is the land which I sware unto Abraham, unto Isaac, and unto Jacob, saying, I will give it unto thy seed: I have caused thee to see it with thine eyes, but thou shalt not go over thither.

So Moses the servant of the Lord died there in the land of Moab, according to the word of the Lord.

And he buried him in a valley in the land of Moab, over against Bethpeor: but no man knoweth of his sepulcher unto this day.

And Moses was a hundred and twenty years old when he died: his eye was not dim, nor his natural force abated.

The spirit of Moses and Elijah both spoke to Jesus before he was crucified at the Transfiguration. One wonders why did God choose Moses and Elijah to speak to Jesus? What did they say to him?

This event was witnessed by Peter, James, and John. They actually saw the spirit of Moses and Elijah along with the Cloud of God, which descended from heaven. According to the Bible, as stated in **Mark 9:2-4 (WEB)**, *After six days Jesus took with him Peter, James, and John, and brought them up onto a high mountain privately by themselves, and he was changed into another form in front of them. His clothing became glistening, exceedingly white, like snow, such as no launderer on earth can whiten them. Elijah and Moses appeared to them, and they were talking with Jesus.*

God spoke to Peter, James, and John as stated in **Mark 9:7 (WEB)**, *A cloud came, overshadowing them,* *and a voice came out of the cloud, "This is my beloved Son. Listen to him."*

After the death of Moses, Joshua led his people back to the land of Canaan, as God promised. Moses was a hero and faithful servant of God. What an amazing person, he must have been.

From here we leap ahead in time from 1400 BC to about 875 BC. It is the time when the kingdom of Israel is divided and a great prophet, Elijah, comes forward, who was appointed by God, to save the country.

THE BOOKS OF KINGS

The Books of Kings (1 and 2) advises the history and prophecy of the divided kingdoms of Israel and Judah. The author is unknown, but it is assumed they were written by the prophet Jeremiah. The Books of Kings covers approximately four hundred years from the time of David, until 586 BC when Jerusalem is destroyed by Nebuchadnezzar. This is when the Ark of the Covenant disappears from the Bible forever. It seems no one knows what happened to it.

There are many key people in the two books that include: Elijah, Elisha, the woman from Shunem, Naaman, Jezebel, Ahab, Jehu, Joash, Hezekiah, Neko, Sennacherib, Isaiah, Manasseh, Josiah, Jehoiakim, Zedekiah, and Nebuchadnezzar. We will only discuss Elijah and Elisha the two key prophets of the time.

The purpose of these books was to advise the

benefits for those who obey God, and the fate of those people who do not obey.

In these books, God performs amazing miracles through his prophets. He sends prophets to spread His Words. The two kingdoms (Israel and Judah) have strayed from the Lord, and are committing the worse possible sins. It's a time of great turmoil and disbelief among the people. God's prophets bring the only hope to help the people change their ways. However, the people do not listen, which greatly upsets the Lord. The star prophets in the Books of Kings are Elijah and Elisha.

Prophet Elijah

Many have probably heard or read about Elijah, one of the great prophets. He was a powerful and fearless man of God who conducted many miracles in the name of the Lord. There are three reasons to mention this man of God. First of all, he never died a normal death. Elijah was raptured or taken by God right in front of his student Elisha. The second reason is that his spirit talked to Jesus right before the crucifixion during the transfiguration. The third is Elijah raised a boy from the dead.

Luke 9:30-31 (WEB), *Behold, two men were talking with him, who were Moses and Elijah, who appeared in glory, and spoke of his departure, which he was about to accomplish at Jerusalem.*

Because of the sins being committed in Israel Elijah

told king Ahab there would be a drought for the next few years because of the king's evil ways. Elijah suddenly appears in the Bible in **1 Kings 17:1 (WEB)**, *Elijah the Tishbite, who was one of the settlers of Gilead, said to Ahab, "As Yahweh, the God of Israel, lives, before whom I stand, there shall not be dew nor rain these years, but according to my word."*

No one knows exactly where Elijah came from, other than from Tishbe in Gilead, which made him a Tishbite. This is in the northern state of the Kingdom of Israel. No other history or background is given in the Bible. His name in Hebrew means "My God Is Yahweh," and his name fits him well. He challenged all those that worshiped false gods like Baal. Baal, at the time, was the main false god being worshiped in Israel. The people had turned their backs on the one true God.

The time period is about 850 BC. Canaan had become two different countries. Israel is the northern part; and the Kingdom of Judah, with Jerusalem (means God is Peace) as its capital, was the southern part. They were not on friendly terms and had many disagreements, especially about worshiping God and taxes.

There are not many direct two-way conversations between God and Elijah written in the Bible. It seems that God does not appear to Elijah in human form. God comes to Elijah in dreams or visions and advises him what to do. Sometimes Elijah uses his own holy instincts and acts freely to make a miracle happen. His faith is so strong that God trusts him to do what is right.

God calls Elijah to come out of the cave and fight

for Him.

1 Kings 19:13-18 (WEB), *When Elijah heard it, he wrapped his face in his mantle, went out, and stood in the entrance of the cave. Behold, a voice came to him, and said, "What are you doing here, Elijah?"*

He said, "I have been very jealous for Yahweh, the God of Armies; for the children of Israel have forsaken your covenant, thrown down your altars, and killed your prophets with the sword. I, even I only, am left; and they seek my life, to take it away."

Yahweh said to him, "Go, return on your way to the wilderness of Damascus. When you arrive, anoint Hazael to be king over Syria. Anoint Jehu the son of Nimshi to be king over Israel; and anoint Elisha the son of Shaphat of Abel Meholah to be prophet in your place. He who escapes from the sword of Hazael, Jehu will kill; and he who escapes from the sword of Jehu, Elisha will kill. Yet I reserved seven thousand in Israel, all the knees of which have not bowed to Baal, and every mouth which has not kissed him."

Jezebel, the Queen of Israel, had put to death most of the Hebrew prophets, and the only one left speaking out in the name of God, was Elijah. Jezebel wanted all her people to worship Baal. Ahab, the king of Israel, and Jezebel were pure evil and had no qualms about killing anyone who disagreed with them. They wanted Elijah dead, but because he was a powerful prophet blessed by the real God, they were afraid to kill him.

As told in the Bible, Elijah challenged all those that did not believe in God. He was bold and direct.

Baal was the Canaanite false god responsible for rain, thunder, lightning, and dew. Elijah not only challenged Baal on behalf of God himself, he challenged Queen Jezebel, Ahab the King, the false priests, and the people of Israel.

King Ahab asked his men in **2 Kings 1:7-10 (WEB)**, *he said to them, "What kind of man was he who came up to meet you, and told you these words?"*

They answered him, "he was a hairy man, and wearing a leather belt around his waist."

He said, "It's Elijah the Tishbite."

Then the king sent a captain of fifty with his fifty to him. He went up to him, and behold, he was sitting on the top of the hill. He said to him, "Man of God, the king has said, 'Come down!'"

Elijah answered to the captain of fifty, "If I am a man of God, then let fire come down from the sky, and consume you and your fifty!" Then fire came down from the sky and consumed him and his fifty.

Elijah performs many miracles healing the sick and brings back the dead. He parts the Jordan River to walk across. He heals people with leprosy. He kills God's enemies in a ruthless manner using God's power that was bestowed upon him.

Elijah is the only person to be picked up by a whirlwind in the Bible and taken to heaven. As witnessed by Elisha, as they walked along together near the Jordan River, a whirlwind appears and suddenly a chariot of fire with flaming horses comes out of the swirling cloud and passes in between them, separating the two men. Elijah is quickly sucked up in the whirlwind right in front of Elisha's eyes. God took him because it was his time to leave earth. Elijah had faithfully served the Lord, and he was ready to pass on to meet his maker.

As Elijah was pulled into the sky on the chariot of fire he dropped his cloak to the ground, and Elisha quickly picked it up. After standing there in disbelief for a while, Elisha proceeded back home but needed to cross the Jordan River along the way. Since he was Elijah's student, Elisha wondered if he would also have the power of God's blessings. Like he saw Elijah do before, he touched the cloak on the Jordan River. And behold, the waters stopped flowing and parted so he could cross on dry land. Some men were standing there watching him, and as they saw the water part they shouted, *"The spirit of Elijah is now resting on Elisha!"*

2 Kings 2:8-15 (WEB), *Elijah took his mantle, and rolled it up, and struck the waters, and they were divided here and there, so that they both went over on dry ground. When they had gone over, Elijah said to Elisha, "Ask what I shall do for you, before I am taken from you."*

Elisha said, "Please let a double portion of your spirit be on me."

He said, "You have asked a hard thing. If you see me when I am taken from you, it will be so for you; but if not, it will not be so."

As they continued on and talked, behold, a chariot

of fire and horses of fire separated them, and Elijah went up by a whirlwind into heaven. Elisha saw it, and he cried, "My father, my father, the chariots of Israel and its horsemen!"

He saw him no more. Then he took hold of his own clothes and tore them in two pieces. He also took up Elijah's mantle that fell from him, and went back, and stood by the bank of the Jordan. He took Elijah's mantle that fell from him, and struck the waters, and said, "Where is Yahweh, the God of Elijah?" When he also had struck the waters, they were divided apart, and Elisha went over. When the sons of the prophets who were at Jericho saw him, they said, "The spirit of Elijah rests on Elisha." They came to meet him and bowed themselves to the ground before him.

Comments

Elijah was sitting on top of the hill waiting for the soldiers to come. He did not run, he did not fear them. He knew the power of God would protect him. His faith in the Lord was strong.

In this story fire rains down on another fifty men, killing them all. A total of one hundred die in a short time span, and Elijah never raised a hand to fight back. God protected him. It can be assumed that the fire was lightning.

So, the king sent another group of fifty to capture Elijah. This captain begged Elijah not to kill them because they were just following orders. An angel from the Lord told Elijah to go with them and be not afraid. Elijah did as the angel said, and went to meet the king. Again, Elijah showed strong faith in following God's directions knowing that the king and queen wanted him dead.

You could very well imagine that the soldiers and the king wouldn't dare to hurt Elijah for fear of being killed by God's power. To unlock God's power, faith is required.

Needless to say, the king and queen do not have a happy ending as told in **1 Kings 21**. King Ahab is killed during a battle at Ramoth, in Gilead, from an arrow to the chest. Jezebel is literally fed to the dogs.

Prophet Elisha

Elijah has been taken by God, and Elisha has become the main prophet of Israel. The first time Elisha is mentioned in the Bible is in **1 Kings 19:16-17 (WEB)**, *Anoint Jehu the son of Nimshi to be king over Israel; and anoint Elisha the son of Shaphat of Abel Meholah to be prophet in your place. He who escapes from the sword of Hazael, Jehu will kill; and he who escapes from the sword of Jehu, Elisha will kill.*

Elijah goes and finds Elisha as told in **1 Kings 19:19 (WEB)**, *So he departed from there, and found Elisha the son of Shaphat, who was plowing with twelve yoke of oxen before him, and he was with the twelfth. Elijah went over to him and put his mantle on him. Elisha left the oxen, and ran after Elijah, and said,*

"Let me please kiss my father and my mother, and then I will follow you."

Elisha becomes just as powerful as his teacher. But will the people listen to him? His name means "God is Salvation."

Elisha was the son of Shaphat, a wealthy land-owner in Abel-meholah. His ministry lasted about sixty years. Elisha becomes a brave and wonderful prophet for God. He was the student of Elijah, and the Lord handpicked him to learn the ways of a prophet. He became the attendant and disciple of Elijah as commanded by God.

He worked his wonders in the northern Kingdom of Israel and was active during the reigns of the following kings: Joram, Jehu, Jehoahaz, and Jehoash.

It was during Elisha's ministry that organized Baal worship was extinguished. The evil leaders of Baal were killed one-by-one by the hand of God. In his ministry, Elisha traveled the country and served as a consultant to kings, and was a friend to all the people.

The miracles Elisha performed were mostly acts of helpfulness such as; the purification of Jericho's contaminated waters, the resurrection of the Shunammite woman's son, and the curing of Naaman's leprosy. Some of Elisha's miracles, such as the multiplication of twenty barley loaves to feed a hundred men, strongly resemble certain miracles of Christ. A study of the life of Elisha reveals the prophet's faithfulness in serving God.

2 Kings 2:19-22 (WEB), *The men of the city said to Elisha, "Behold, please, the situation of this city is pleasant, as my lord sees; but the water is bad, and the land is barren."*

He said, "Bring me a new jar, and put salt in it." Then they brought it to him. He went out to the spring of the waters, and threw salt into it, and said, "Yahweh says, 'I have healed these waters. There shall not be from there any more death or barren wasteland.'" So, the waters were healed to this day, according to Elisha's word which he spoke.

2 Kings 4:32-35 (WEB), *When Elisha had come into the house, behold, the child was dead and lying on his bed. He went in therefore, and shut the door on them both, and prayed to Yahweh. He went up, and lay on the child, and put his mouth on his mouth, and his eyes on his eyes, and his hands on his hands. He stretched himself on him, and the child's flesh grew warm. Then he returned, and walked in the house once back and forth; and went up, and stretched himself out on him. Then the child sneezed seven times, and the child opened his eyes.*

2 Kings 4:42-44 (WEB), *A man from Baal Shalishah came, and brought the man of God bread and some of the first fruits: twenty loaves of barley, and fresh ears of grain in his sack. He said, "Give to the people, that they may eat."*

His servant said, "What, should I set this before a hundred men?"

But he said, "Give the people, that they may eat;

for Yahweh says, 'They will eat, and will have some left over.'"

So he set it before them, and they ate, and had some left over, according to Yahweh's word.

2 Kings 13:14 (WEB), *Now Elisha became sick with the illness of which he died; and Joash the king of Israel came down to him, and wept over him, and said, "My father, my father, the chariots of Israel and its horsemen!"*

Comments

The main noteworthy accomplishment for Elisha was the fact that the worship of Baal was eliminated in Canaan by him, with the help of God. He was a brave and fearless warrior and believer in the Lord. It seems God gave him the ability to use his own judgment most of the time. He was a doer and acted quickly to deal out justice and miracles. He was a knight in shining armor fighting evil and doing good deeds. His faith in the Lord was very strong.

God granted Elisha the same powers that Elijah had. Among these was the power to raise the dead, when it was deemed proper to do so. Both of these prophets used that power once during their lives.

Others Who Saw or Spoke to God

In the Old Testament the following people are commonly listed as having seen or spoken with God:

Solomon, Job, Isaiah, Micaiah, Jeremiah, Ezekiel, King Nebuchadnezzar, Shadrach, Meshach, Daniel, Amos, Jonah, Habakkuk, King Neko, Cyrus King of Persia, and Zechariah.

The key point of this section (Old Testament People Who Saw and/or Spoke to God) is that all these people had one thing in common, they believed in the Lord. They all followed God's commands without question. Even the enemies of the Jews, King Nebuchadnezzar, King Cyrus, and King Neko of Egypt, followed God's commands. Why would the so-called enemies of the Jews listen to God if he were not real? They feared God's power and knew that He was real.

Conclusion

The Old Testament ends with the Book of Malachi. The following are the very last Scripture verses.

Malachi 4:4-6 (WEB), *"Remember the law of Moses my servant, which I commanded to him in Horeb for all Israel, even statutes and ordinances. Behold, I will send you Elijah the prophet before the great and terrible day of Yahweh comes. He will turn the hearts of the fathers to the children, and the hearts of the children to their fathers, lest I come and strike the earth with a curse."*

From here we jump ahead in time to the birth of Christ. Next is the New Covenant, Jesus, and the New Testament, and the amazing disciples who spread the word and started the foundations of the church.

THOMAS H. WARD

CHAPTER 5

THE COVENANTS

We are now leaping ahead in time by over five hundred years. The Son of God has been born, and a New Covenant has been made with the Lord. During this time span, Jerusalem has been destroyed and rebuilt. Since 62 BC the Romans have controlled Israel and all its lands.

The Old Covenant

As arranged by God, the Jews had a long history of paying for their sins by offering blood sacrifices using animals. God set up the sacrificial system of accepting the death of animals as a substitute for the taking of human life for those that sinned. It seems that God considered most sins to be a major offense.

The Old Covenant was summed up in the Book of Laws written by Moses, but provided by God. That was part of God's agreement with the Hebrews in ancient times.

Leviticus 17:11 (KJV), *For the life of the flesh is in the blood: and I have given it to you upon the altar to make an atonement for your souls: for it is the blood that maketh an atonement for the soul.*

The New Covenant

With the advent of Jesus, God also brought forth a New Covenant for all of mankind. God sacrificed his only Son to help cleanse us from our sins. The New Covenant comes through the death of Jesus Christ.

What does the Bible mean when it talks about a New Covenant between us and God? The New Covenant is the ultimate solution to forgive people for their sins. The New Covenant means we will go directly to God through Christ. This Covenant is meant for everyone and not just those of Jewish faith.

Luke 22:19-20 (WEB), *he took bread, and when he had given thanks, he broke it, and gave to them, saying, "This is my body which is given for you. Do this in memory of me." Likewise, he took the cup after supper, saying, "This cup is the new covenant in my blood, which is poured out for you."*

Hebrews 1: 1-4 (WEB), *God, having in the past spoken to the fathers through the prophets at many times and in various ways, has at the end of these days spoken to us by his Son, whom he appointed heir of all things, through whom also he made the worlds. His Son is the radiance of his glory, the very image of his substance, and upholding all things by the word of his power, when* *he had by himself purified us of our sins, sat down on the right hand of the Majesty on high; having become so much better than the angels, as he has inherited a more excellent name than they have.*

Comments

Jesus Christ is here; the Son of God has come to save everyone from our sins and to help us believe in Almighty God. Our Lord and Savior has given you the ability to have faith, if you choose to do so.

THOMÁS H. WARD

CHAPTER 6

JESUS and
THE NEW TESTAMENT

Most people know the story of Jesus, the Son of God. He is, without a doubt, the most famous and important being that has ever walked on this earth. People know how he was born, how he died, how he was resurrected, and then went to be with our Father Almighty.

John 17:1-3 (WEB), *Jesus said these things, and lifting up his eyes to heaven, he said, "Father, the time has come. Glorify your Son, that your Son may also glorify you; even as you gave him authority over all flesh, he will give eternal life to all whom you have given him. This is eternal life, that they should know you, the only true God, and him whom you sent, Jesus Christ."*

Jesus had a huge following of believers because of all the good deeds he did. We know that Jesus used two major methods to teach the New Covenant and to prove he was the Son of God. One was by preaching and the other was by using miracles to heal the sick. Not only does he heal the sick, but he raises the dead. This happens more than one time in the New Testament. These incredible miracles were witnessed by his disciples and thousands of people.

Jesus heals the sick, as stated in **Matthew 4:23-25 (WEB)**, *Jesus went about in all Galilee, teaching in their synagogues, preaching the Good News of the Kingdom, and healing every disease and every sickness among the people. The report about him went out into all Syria. They brought to him all who were sick, afflicted with various diseases and torments, possessed by demons, epileptics, and paralytics; and he healed them. Great multitudes from Galilee, Decapolis, Jerusalem, Judea, and from beyond the Jordan followed him.*

There are very interesting facts and stories that people don't know about Jesus, his disciples, and the Bible. Read further to find out something new, wonderful, and mysterious about the ancient days. It should be noted that all the books in the New Testament were written years after Christ had ascended to the Father. However, written letters and scrolls were recorded at the time, which would later be used to make up the New Testament.

Two thousand years ago Jesus walked the earth and we know his name today. We know his good deeds and something about his life. The world population has ballooned to seven billion people. More than a third of them are self-proclaimed Christians, according to a survey taken in 2016. There are more Christians than any other religion. Jesus and his disciples did an amazing job of spreading the word. It was all in God's plan that every Christian would be a witness and help propagate the Word of God.

John 11:25-26 (WEB), *Jesus said to her, "I am the resurrection and the life. He who believes in me will still live, even if he dies. Whoever lives and believes in me will never die. Do you believe this?"*

However, Jesus is still a mystery to us all and especially to those who do not believe. Believers who have faith accept that we may never understand exactly what happened two thousand years ago. Also, we certainly have no exact idea what will happen when we die. But we have faith and try to follow the teachings of Christ.

What does it take for non-believers to accept that Jesus is the Son of God? Sadly, some people will never become believers, and God calls them *"stiff-necked people."* It takes faith to believe, which God has given you. You can accept and believe in Christ by using your faith or not. The choice is up to you. Choose wisely and you may be able to unlock the power of God.

Matthew 16:13-16 (WEB), *Now when Jesus came into the parts of Caesarea Philippi, He asked his disciples, saying, "Who do men say that I, the Son of Man, am?"*

They said, "Some say John the Baptizer, some, Elijah, and others, Jeremiah, or one of the prophets."

He said to them, "But who do you say that I am?"

Simon Peter answered, "You are the Christ, the Son of the living God."

Ancient prophets preached, years ahead of time, that God would send a Messiah who would bring peace to Israel and the known world at that time.

Jeremiah 31:31 (WEB), *"Behold, the days come, says Yahweh, that I will make a new covenant with the house of Israel, and with the house of Judah."*

It has been six hundred years since the last king of the Hebrews. Rome has ruled Judae for the last hundred years. Jesus has been born. Living under the rule of Rome wasn't easy. The people were being heavily taxed and forced to do Rome's bidding.

The Old Covenant rested in the Book of Laws written from the time of Moses. The new agreement, which is the New Covenant, is between God and his people. Jesus would come as the Messiah and would teach the people up close, face-to-face. He would appoint disciples to follow his lead and help spread the Word of God around the known world at the time.

The main problem was that Jesus didn't fully meet the expectations of all the Jews to be the Messiah. They were expecting a warrior who would free them from Rome. Instead, Jesus was a pacifist. Why did God send his Son to be a person who showed comfort and love instead of violence and hate? Why did God send a healer instead of a warrior who would do battle? These were the questions raised in ancient days by the leaders of the Jews, who had disobeyed God's commandments many times. They couldn't understand what God was doing and didn't believe because of their own greed.

Who were the Twelve Disciples? What do we know about them? Who were Matthew, Mark, Luke, and John? Who wrote the New Testament Books? Continue reading to discover who these people were, and what impact they had on the Bible Scriptures. We will learn why Jesus chose these men and women to spread the Word of God. Women played an important part throughout the Bible and in spreading the words of Jesus.

Perhaps we can answer the above questions by reading the New Testament. It becomes clear that God has given all authority to his Son Jesus Christ. It is clear that a new tone is being set for all of humankind and not just with the people of Jewish faith. The next section covers little-known facts about Jesus and the people he knew.

Little Known Facts About Jesus and Those He Knew

Eight days after his birth, Joseph and Mary took baby Jesus to the local synagogue to be blessed and circumcised. As stated in **Luke 2:28-32 (WEB)**, *then he received him into his arms, and blessed God, and said, "Now you are releasing your servant, Master, according to your word, in peace; for my eyes have seen your salvation, which you have prepared before the face of all peoples; a light for revelation to the nations, and the glory of your people Israel."*

Simeon, the Jewish priest, who held Jesus and did

the circumcision, knew right away that Jesus was the Son of God, and would bless all people whether they were Jewish or not.

*****

Isaiah 19:25 (WEB), *because Yahweh of Armies has blessed them, saying, "Blessed be Egypt my people, Assyria the work of my hands, and Israel my inheritance."*

Isaiah, the prophet, advised 700 years earlier that God had plans for Egypt, Assyria, and Israel. They were to be linked together and united under God Almighty.

When I was doing research for this book a friend of mine who is a Coptic Christian gave me a book on the travels of Joseph, Mary, and baby Jesus when they fled Bethlehem from King Herod and went to Egypt for safety. This short book was written in Arabic, Greek, and Old English. The title is *"The Flight of the Holy Family to Egypt."* This is written from ancient Coptic records by Faty Saiid Georgy and was introduced by Bishop Mettaos of the Saint Mary Syrian Monastery. Only three detailed copies of the original document are known to exist today.

Matthew 2:13 (WEB), *Now when they had departed, behold, an angel of the Lord appeared to Joseph in a dream, saying, "Arise and take the young child and his mother, and flee into Egypt, and stay there until I tell you, for Herod will seek the young child to destroy him."*

The Bible gives no details of their estimated three-year long journey that took them throughout Egypt. Actually, it's not exactly known how long the family was in Egypt. They were poor Jews and had no or little money. They entered the land that had once used the Hebrews for slaves. Why did the angel of God tell them to go to Egypt? How did they live and obtain food? Who helped them in this foreign land?

Note: *"Coptic" means "Egyptian"; therefore, Christians in Egypt identify themselves as Coptic Christians. The first Church was started in the city of Alexandria, one of the most faithful, and powerful, cities during ancient times. Coptic Christians state that Mark (author of the Gospel of Mark) was the founder of the Church around AD 42–62. The Coptic Church has its own version of the Bible as well as other ancient Scriptures and books providing a history only known to those in the Coptic Church.*

When the Holy Family went to Egypt it was a long and dangerous journey. Who went with them, if anyone? They were poor, and the only items they had of any value were those gifts given to them by the three Wise Men. It can be assumed that these generous gifts helped pay for the trip. The Coptic story doesn't say who was with them or offer any detail in the short book. It does state, however, that when little Jesus entered a city that had exposed idols of the Egyptian gods, they would topple to the ground and break in half as Jesus passed by. This happened in city after city. Word quickly spread that this was a Holy Family with powers beyond reason.

The book covers the fact that the Christ family traveled to twenty-five different locations throughout Egypt. Word spread and they were widely accepted by the people. The local people provided food and housing. They could tell that little Jesus was something special and holy.

Matthew 2:19 (WEB), *But when Herod was dead, behold, an angel of the Lord appeared in a dream to Joseph in Egypt, saying, "Arise and take the young child and his mother, and go into the land of Israel, for those who sought the young child's life are dead."*

Years later hundreds of churches sprang up along the route that Jesus had followed. As stated earlier, Mark was the person who started the Coptic Church. Christians were very numerous in the ancient times after Jesus rose to be with the Father. Christianity spread like wild-fire across Egypt, and the Coptic Church grew.

One needs to remember that the Egyptians and the Hebrews had a long history of living together. Many Hebrews still lived in Egypt from the slave days. The belief in one true God, the God of Abraham, was strong among some Egyptians, who were actively trading goods with the Israelites and at times would intermarry. Thus, many of the Egyptian people could relate to a Messiah being born. They had faith that Christ would save the world.

*****

Did you know that Jesus had four brothers and two or three sisters? Yes, what a shock! Some scholars dismiss the fact that he had brothers, but the New Testament clearly states that he did. As stated in **Matthew 13:55 (WEB)**, "*Isn't this the carpenter's son? Isn't his mother called Mary, and his brothers, James, Joses, Simon, and Jude (Judas)?*"

According to some ancient records, his sisters' names were, Miriam, Martha, and Ruth. In other stories, there were two sisters named Lysia and Lydia. Some believe these were step-brothers and step-sisters of Jesus and that Joseph was married before, thereby making them older. This is a debatable subject since the Bible does not mention that Joseph was married before and already had children from another wife, who had passed away.

Also, there is no mention of these brothers and sisters when the family went to Bethlehem for the census taking. They surely would have had to go as a family with their father, under the requirement of Roman law. There is no mention of them when Mary and Joseph fled to Egypt to save the life of baby Jesus. There is no mention of them in the few stories relating to when Jesus was a child. These siblings are not mentioned in the Bible until Jesus is an adult.

This means that the brothers and sisters were most likely born to Mary and Joseph after the birth of Jesus and were slightly younger. Yes, Joseph was their father, but God was the Father of Jesus. After the Virgin Mary gave birth to Christ it would be natural for Joseph and Mary to want more children. Certainly, God would bless them, so they could multiply. In those days the more children you had the better it was for the family unit.

The Bible doesn't state that Mary never had any more children after Jesus was born. You can decide which theory is correct. No one actually knows, so this is a controversial subject.

We should note that technically speaking, the siblings of Jesus were his half-brothers and sisters. It is clear that the Father of Jesus was the Holy Spirit (God), and not Joseph. So, they had the same mother but different fathers. Of course, Mary and Joseph knew this fact, but no one else knew Jesus was the Son of God until Christ was older and started preaching the Word of God. It was probably then that Mary told the real story of Jesus to his siblings. She told them that Jesus, their brother, was actually the Son of God. That must have been a real shock to them. Please keep reading because there is further evidence that Jesus had brothers as mentioned in other scriptures and ancient texts.

Christ's brothers at first did not believe he was the Son of God. They were converted to believers after they witnessed the miracles of Jesus. His brother James wrote the Book of James and was the leader of the first Jerusalem Church. It is stated in **James 1 (WEB)**, *James, a servant of God and of the Lord Jesus Christ, to the twelve tribes which are in the Dispersion: Greetings.*

As a leader in Jerusalem, James spoke with authority to end an internal Church dispute over the circumcision of Gentile believers **(Acts 15:13–19 or 21:18)**.

According to a first-century Jewish historian named

Josephus, the Jewish religious hierarchy put to death by stoning *"the brother of Jesus, who was called Christ, whose name was James"* (***Antiquities of the Jews* 20.200**). This would have happened around AD 62. This clearly states Jesus had a brother named James, who was stoned to death by the angry Jewish leaders.

There is some disagreement if James was really an apostle since he is never mentioned directly in the New Testament as a disciple. But this is not correct. Paul, who was an apostle, but wasn't of the Twelve, mentioned James when writing about one of his visits to Jerusalem. **Galatians 1:19 (WEB)**, *"But none of the other apostles I saw no one, except James, the Lord's brother."*

Once again proof is provided in the writings of Paul above. "I saw no one, except James, the Lord's brother."

His brother Jude, wrote the Book of Jude. Please note that this is not the same Judas that betrayed Christ. From **Jude 1 (WEB)**, *Jude, a servant of Jesus Christ, and brother of James, to those who are called, sanctified by God the Father, and kept for Jesus Christ: Mercy to you and peace and love be multiplied.*

If Jude is the brother of James then he is also the brother of Jesus. James and Jude became disciples to help spread the Good News. Other than this information, there are no other details about Jesus' brothers. It's interesting that neither brother mentions in their writings that Jesus was their actual brother. One cannot help but wonder why. Maybe it was because being a supporter and believer in Jesus as the Messiah was dangerous.

Maybe they were trying to protect their family from the wrath of the Jewish leaders. Maybe it was out of respect for the Son of God, who was their half-brother.

The Bible does not mention what His other two brothers (Joses and Simon) actually did, but one can assume they were involved somehow in helping to spread the Good News. There is no mention of what His sisters did to aid him, or anything about them. Most likely they were married and were not involved in the activities of Jesus, but we don't know for sure.

There is still disagreement within the Holy Community whether Jesus had brothers and sisters who were born of Mary and Joseph. There is no real proof other than what is written in the Bible. These are God's Words. It is left up to each of us to decide what to believe. There is, however, further Scripture evidence that Jesus did have half-brothers in the upcoming sections.

*****

Little is known about Joseph the earthly father of Jesus. It is believed that Joseph died during the unknown years of Jesus' life. We do know he trained Jesus to be a carpenter since that was his trade. Some believe that Joseph and Mary had other children after Jesus was born: James, Joses (Joseph), Simon, Jude, and two or three daughters. The last reference about Joseph in **Luke** confirms that he was a devout follower and believer in God. He observed the customs of his Jewish religion. It also can be assumed that Joseph was a good father. Joseph proved his willingness to be obedient to God's direction when he was chosen to take Mary as his wife.

It is thought that Joseph was a good deal older than Mary and that he died before Jesus began his ministry. We know that Joseph was not there when Jesus was killed on the cross. The body of Jesus was taken charge of by Joseph of Arimathea, a role his father would have taken on if he were still alive. The father that God chose for Jesus just disappears from the Bible Scriptures. It is said that Joseph passed on when he was 111 years old, but this is not actually known. To find out more about Joseph refer to "The History of Joseph the Carpenter" in articles on the internet.

We only know that Joseph did his best to raise Jesus. He did what God directed him to do without question, because of his strong faith.

Who was Joseph of Arimathea? What connection did he have to Jesus? Continue reading and we will find out something important about this man. It is something amazing and not known to most people. We will discover who Joseph of Arimathea was, but first, let's review a few more amazing facts about Jesus.

*****

We actually know very little about the mother of Jesus. What happened to Mary the loyal servant of God when Christ rose to the Father? The Apostle John (the beloved disciple) wrote in **John 19:25-27 (KJV)**, *Now there stood by the cross of Jesus his mother, and his mother's sister, Mary the wife of Cleophas, and Mary Magdalene.*

When Jesus therefore saw his mother, and the

disciple standing by, whom he loved, he saith unto his mother, Woman, behold thy son!

Then saith he to the disciple, Behold thy mother! And from that hour that disciple took her unto his own home.

Note that Jesus no longer calls Mary his mother but calls her "Woman," which means Mary is no longer seen as His mother. Jesus is now Mary's Lord and Savior. Also, Jesus charges Apostle John to take care of Mary since he can no longer do so.

This is another important clue that Jesus was older than his brothers and sisters. It was always the oldest son who took care of the mother after her husband died. The oldest son, even if in the grasp of death, decided what would happen to his Mother. However, it could also mean that Mary was not the mother of his brothers so they felt no obligation to take care of her. We don't know why Jesus did this but there was a reason, which needless to say, eludes us.

But why didn't the brothers of Jesus take care of Mary? We can assume that they did help Mary. However, we can also conclude they were not at the cross-watching Jesus die, either out of fear for their own lives or they simply could not watch the horrible event. Maybe they did watch from a distance, but this is speculation. In any case, Jesus was concerned about the wellbeing of his mother, and appointed the disciple he loved to take care of her.

The very last mention in the Scriptures of Mary (the mother of Jesus) is in **Acts 1:13-14 (WEB)**, *When they* *had come in, they went up into the upper room, where they were staying; that is Peter, John, James, Andrew, Philip, Thomas, Bartholomew, Matthew, James the son of Alphaeus, Simon the Zealot, and Judas the son of James. All these with one accord continued steadfastly in prayer and supplication, along with the women, and Mary the mother of Jesus, and with his brothers.*

This proves that Mary had joined with the disciples, as well as His brothers, and were part of the early Church. We don't know how much longer she lived because the Bible doesn't say. In conclusion, we just don't know what happened to Mary after the crucifixion. We do know she became part of the new church and that the Apostle John cared for her. It is said that John and Mary later moved to Ephesus, a city located in modern Turkey. More information is revealed in a later chapter called "The Women Disciples." This chapter reveals what may have happened to Mary.

*****

Most people don't know that Jesus made the little village of Capernaum his home during the years of his ministry.

Matthew 4:13 (WEB), *Leaving Nazareth, he came and lived in Capernaum, which is by the sea, in the region of Zebulun and Naphtali.*

Capernaum is a key city in Galilee, where he met most of his loyal disciples. So, he had good reasons for moving to Capernaum. When Jesus heard that John the Baptist was delivered up, he withdrew to Galilee to preach.

Matthew 4:12-17 (WEB), *Now when Jesus heard that John was delivered up, he withdrew into Galilee. Leaving Nazareth, he came and lived in Capernaum, which is by the sea, in the region of Zebulun and Naphtali, that it might be fulfilled which was spoken through Isaiah the prophet, saying, "The land of Zebulun and the land of Naphtali, toward the sea, beyond the Jordan, Galilee of the Gentiles, the people who sat in darkness saw a great light, to those who sat in the region and shadow of death, to them light has dawned."*

John was beheaded, and from these times on Jesus began to preach. He told everyone, "Repent! For the Kingdom of Heaven is at hand."

The above Isaiah prophecy is one of the reasons Jesus went to Capernaum to live. Jesus was fulfilling what the prophet Isaiah had forecasted about six hundred years earlier.

Luke 4:31-36 (WEB), *He came down to Capernaum, a city of Galilee. He was teaching them on the Sabbath day, and they were astonished at his teaching, for his word was with authority. In the synagogue, there was a man who had a spirit of an unclean demon, and he cried out with a loud voice, saying, "Ah! What have we to do with you, Jesus of Nazareth? Have you come to destroy us? I know you who you are: The Holy One of God!"*

Jesus rebuked him, saying, "Be silent, and come out of him!" When the demon had thrown him down in the middle of them, he came out of him, having done him no harm.

Amazement came on all, and they spoke together, one with another, saying, "What is this word? For with authority and power, he commands the unclean spirits, and they come out!"

News about him went out into every place of the surrounding region.

From that time, Jesus began to preach, and conduct more miracles. The people started to follow him and they asked for his blessings.

Many do not realize that Jesus actually only preached for a little more than three years. Of course, during His entire lifetime, He always performed miracles and spoke about the Scriptures and there meaning. It is estimated that Jesus lived here on earth until his mid-thirties.

There is another reason that Jesus chose Capernaum to live in, but that will be discussed in a later section. It was because of the people living there. They were sinners who were seeking God.

*****

The Jewish leaders and enforcers of the law hated Jesus and wanted him dead. They feared the people would turn away from the old ways. They didn't want to believe in Christ and the New Covenant he was teaching. So, they plotted to kill him.

Thousands of Jews started to believe that Jesus was the Son of God. As more and more people came to

Christ the Jewish leaders became very upset and needed to stop Jesus somehow, so they made their plans. Little did they know, that it was God's plan they were going to activate.

Who were these Jewish leaders? The ruling religious and legal authorities were the Sanhedrin. This was the ruling council composed of seventy men. They were chief priests, scribes, and elders of Judea. The high priest served as the group's leader. They arbitrated all criminal, civil, and religious law. The Sanhedrin had their own police and enforced the law with fines and imprisonment. However, they were not permitted to impose the death penalty on anyone. This was only administered by the Roman governor.

The Sanhedrin most likely consisted of men who were also members of the Sadducees and Pharisees. Simply put the Sadducees were the ruling elite who cooperated with the Romans and rejected the ideas of angels and resurrection of the dead.

The Pharisees were an opposing group, since they had more liberal beliefs. However, they strictly upheld Jewish laws and fabricated rules that were unreasonable for the people to follow.

You may ask, "Why didn't these leaders believe?" The answer is simple: greed and power were the main reasons. The Jewish priests would have lost their authority, power, and money under the New Covenant. They were locked into the Old Testament and man-made Jewish laws. They could not believe that God had, at last, sent the Messiah. Most refused to even debate the subject. God knew they would act this way.

All believers know our Savior is Jesus Christ and He is the Son of God. We know of His good works and blessings. Jesus had the ultimate faith in the Father Almighty. He lived as a man and therefore had the same feelings as common people do. He could relate to normal people, and that is what made him so effective. That is why God chose to use His Son and have him born as a human on earth.

*****

Jesus raised people from the dead. Many people witnessed this and so did his disciples. He only did this in certain situations, when he was moved to do so. The following story needs to be told because Jesus usually did this in private with just a couple of disciples. This time, however, he raised Lazarus in front of hundreds of people who witnessed the event so the news would spread quickly. Christ wanted as many people as possible to witness this miracle.

There was no doubt that Lazarus was dead since the funeral had been conducted and he had been dead for four days. This was a very important point as there would be no question that Jesus raised him from the dead. It was not a trick of some kind, as the Jewish leaders thought.

His friend, and a disciple, named Lazarus was sick and passed away before Jesus could attend to his illness. It made Jesus cry that his friend had passed away. Lazarus had two sisters, Mary of Bethany, and Martha who were strong believers and had faith in Jesus. Jesus arrived too late as Lazarus was already dead for four days. The miracle is in **John 11:38-44 (KJV)**, *Jesus therefore again groaning in himself cometh to the grave. It was a cave, and a stone lay upon it.*

Jesus said, Take ye away the stone.

Martha, the sister of him that was dead, saith unto him, Lord, by this time he stinketh: for he hath been dead four days.

Jesus saith unto her, Said I not unto thee, that, if thou wouldest believe, thou shouldest see the glory of God?

Then they took away the stone from the place where the dead was laid. And Jesus lifted up his eyes, and said, Father, I thank thee that thou hast heard me.

And I knew that thou hearest me always: but because of the people which stand by I said it, that they may believe that thou hast sent me.

And when he thus had spoken, he cried with a loud voice, Lazarus, come forth.

And he that was dead came forth, bound hand and foot with graveclothes: and his face was bound about with a napkin. Jesus saith unto them, loose him and let him go.

Lazarus and his sisters had great faith in Jesus and knew he was the Son of God. This event was witnessed by many people. The word spread like wildfire about the power of Jesus. Of course, this made his enemies even more determined to kill him. The Jewish leaders did not believe that Jesus was bringing the dead back to life. Only God could do that. They still didn't understand that he was the Son of God.

*****

Joseph of Arimathea was a secret disciple of Jesus. He believed in Christ and did what he could to be of service to him. But he feared his fellow Jews and did not openly demonstrate his belief until Jesus died on the cross.

Matthew 27:57-61 (WEB), *"When evening had come, a rich man from Arimathea, named Joseph, who himself was also Jesus' disciple came. This man went to Pilate and asked for Jesus' body. Then Pilate commanded the body to be given up. Joseph took the body, and wrapped it in a clean linen cloth, and laid it in his own new tomb, which he had cut out in the rock, and he rolled a great stone to the door of the tomb and departed. Mary Magdalene was there, and the other Mary, sitting opposite the tomb."*

The body of Jesus was taken charge of by Joseph of Arimathea, a role that his father would have normally done if he were alive. The fact that Joseph went to Pilate and asked for the body of Christ is a very important point which is often overlooked. Jesus knew this man and knew him very well. He was in the ruling elite of the Jewish higher-ups. He had power and was rich. There are many stories about this man and it is clear he was respected. He showed no fear when he requested the body of Christ be given to him. He was one of the Jewish council members according to **Mark 15:43 (WEB)**, *Joseph of Arimathea, a prominent council* *member who also himself was looking for God's Kingdom, came. He boldly went to Pilate and asked for Jesus' body.*

When Pilate learned from the centurion that Jesus was dead he gave the body to Joseph.

Mark 15:46-47 (WEB), *"he bought a linen cloth, and taking him down, wound him in the linen cloth, and laid him in a tomb which had been cut out of a rock. He rolled a stone against the door of the tomb. Mary Magdalene and Mary, the mother of Joses, saw where he was laid."*

The Bible confirms and states in **John 19:38-39 (WEB)**, *After these things, Joseph of Arimathea, being a disciple of Jesus, but secretly for fear of the Jews, asked of Pilate that he might take away Jesus' body. Pilate gave him permission. He came therefore and took away his body. Nicodemus, who at first came to Jesus by night, also came bringing a mixture of myrrh and aloes, about a hundred Roman pounds.*

Who was Pontius Pilate? He was the ruling governor of Judea appointed by the emperor of Rome, Tiberius, in AD 26. His hatred for the Jews was well known, as was his brutality and lack of empathy. In turn, the Jews hated him and Jerusalem was on the verge of a revolt.

The burial stories of Jesus vary slightly in details from Matthew, Mark, Luke, and John. It is clear Joseph and Nicodemus took the body of Jesus and covered it as Jewish customs dictated when he was taken off the cross. A small cloth (sudarium) covering the face would have been placed on the head and then a large shroud was immediately placed over the entire body to cover it from view. These cloths were supplied by Joseph.

The body was placed in a new tomb that Joseph had specially made for himself sometime earlier. The women, including Mary, followed Joseph to the tomb. They witnessed how his body was laid in it. Since it was almost dark, time for the Sabbath to start, they didn't have time to wash, clean, and prepare the body with spices. They went home to gather the spices and perfume to return in the morning. However, since the next day was the Sabbath they rested and did nothing to the body in obedience to Jewish law.

Joseph was friends with Nicodemus who was a Jewish scholar and one of the leaders on the ruling council known as the Pharisees. They would create and enforce Jewish laws. Late one-night Nicodemus had paid a visit to Jesus. He went in the dark, so no other council members would see him. According to **John 3:2-3 (WEB)**, *The same came to him by night, and said to him, "Rabbi, we know that you are a teacher coming from God, for no one can do these signs that you do, unless God is with him."*

Jesus answered him, "Most certainly, I tell you, unless one is born anew, he can't see God's Kingdom."

That night Jesus taught Nicodemus about being saved and about God. Nicodemus became a believer in secret. He didn't have the courage to speak up to the other members of the Pharisees.

Now here is the interesting part of the story. Note

that it was originally the tomb of Joseph. He was a rich man so the tomb had to be well made, and it was in a good location because he had enough money to buy the best. The location is where the tomb is situated today, thanks to Joseph of Arimathea. In AD 300 The Church of the Holy Sepulchre was built over the tomb. The Edicule (from the Latin word *aedicule*, or "little house"), a structure within The Church of the Holy Sepulchre, encloses a cave that has been accepted, since before the fourth century, as the tomb of Jesus Christ.

As noted, inside the Edicule is the tomb of Christ. Over the years some have questioned if this was really the location of the tomb. Recently the Edicule had reconstruction done due to it its age. During the process, for the first time since around AD 300, the tomb was opened to check for damage. It was possible to view the stone slab where the body of Christ had once lay. The same stone slab from which Jesus arose from the dead.

No one in modern times, and for almost 1,800 years, has seen the slab. After removing the marble cover, which protected the slab, everyone was shocked to see a small Cross, neatly engraved into the slab of stone. Scientific dating has verified the age of the tomb. No one knows how the engraved cross came to be on the stone slab. There is little doubt that this is the tomb that held the body of Christ until he was resurrected.

It is clear that Joseph brought the linen cloths to cover the body of Christ and worked with Nicodemus to move the body, in a holy manner, to the tomb. Both men were believers in Christ. None of the disciples are mentioned as being involved in the moving of his body. Not even his brothers are mentioned, which is indeed strange.

The body of Christ was covered with a linen cloth in Jewish tradition. One smaller cloth covered the face and a larger one, or shroud, covered the body head to toe. This was the general practice until a proper burial could be conducted when the body would be wrapped. The body would not have been tightly wrapped until it was cleaned and spices were applied. When moving the body from the cross to the tomb it would have been simply covered, as we do now in modern days.

The body of Jesus was placed in the tomb by Joseph and Nicodemus. This was witnessed by Mary, the mother of Jesus, and the other women who were at the cross. It was now dark and they could not proceed to clean the body. Also, the next day was the Sabbath, so they could not do the necessary preparation until the third day. But before the women could return to clean the body and prepare it with spices, oils, and perfumes the body of Christ rose from the dead.

Early on the first day of the week (Sunday) Mary and Mary Magdalene went to the tomb and found the body of Christ was gone. They ran to tell Peter and the others. Then, Peter and the beloved one (John) ran to the tomb to see. John, out-ran Peter but did not go inside until Peter came, as stated below in **John**.

John 20:6-7 (WEB), *Then Simon Peter came, following him, and entered into the tomb. He saw the linen cloths lying, and the cloth that had been on his* *head, not lying with the linen cloths, but rolled up in a place by itself.*

It states that the burial cloth that had covered Christ's head was folded up and placed aside. Who did this and why? Why is this small detail even mentioned in the Scriptures? Who cared about the cloth so much? Why was it mentioned that Joseph even supplied a burial cloth? The cloth is something that would have been taken for granted. The Bible leaves out many details, but for some reason, the detail about the cloth is mentioned more than once. Does it not seem odd?

Now, what happened to the burial cloths that covered his face and body? Did Simon Peter pick up the burial cloths? Did Mary, the mother of Jesus, pick them up or did John pick them up? It makes a lot of sense that someone would pick them up. Or did they leave them there? I doubt they left them on the ground for anyone else to take. These items had covered the Son of God, so they were considered to be holy.

Based on the story from the Bible the cloths were in the tomb, but what happened to these linens? That is the question. They were originally the property of Joseph. Certainly, someone picked these up and took them. They covered the Holy Body of Christ and were very important relics. Remember that Mary was now being taken care of by John the beloved one. Later you will see why this is important.

It is possible that Mary, the mother of Jesus, took them, which makes the most sense. These linens were the only possessions she had to remind her of Jesus.

Possibly, Jesus neatly folded the cloth up or an angel did, leaving it for Mary. The fact that it was folded also meant that His body had not been stolen by grave robbers. They would not have taken the time to do such a thing.

Any proof of the resurrection had to be destroyed by the enemies of Christ. Relics were guarded and closely kept secrets. It makes one wonder what happened to these important Holy relics.

*****

Have you ever heard of The Shroud of Turin and The Sudarium of Oviedo? These two pieces of cloth have images embedded in them. The smaller cloth (Sudarium), which covered just the head and face, has bloodstains that match the exact locations and type of blood (type AB), which is also found on the Shroud. Both of them clearly show the small blood spots from a crown of thorns.

The Shroud bears an image of a person complete with blood stains. Viewing the Shroud in a photo negative, one can clearly see the image of a man. A man with blood stains where nails went through his hands and feet. Blood stains were on his side, where he was pierced by some type of weapon. These holy relics are believed to be the linens that covered Jesus. The Shroud is the most highly examined relic in the world. No one knows how the image was made. It is not painted, or anything that is traceable even today. It is a great mystery.

It is believed that this image was caused by a very

bright intense light which could have come from the energy used by God to resurrect Christ. It is estimated that to make this image the light energy would have to be similar in brightness to that being emitted from an atomic bomb. We are just speaking about the brightness of the light and not of an explosion. Jesus was being brought back to life by the energy of God bursting down on his body, and it actually took a negative picture, leaving an image on the white cloth. At least that is the theory.

It wasn't until 1898 that this image was seen in full detail when the first picture of the Shroud was taken. During the development of the black-and-white picture, the photographer looked at the negative and was shocked. He saw the face and body of Jesus Christ. The full image details can only be seen on the negative of a picture and cannot be seen on the shroud directly. The image looks like a sketch of Jesus himself, similar to most typical pictures of Christ. Showing this to the priests in charge of this holy relic, they were also shocked and could not understand how this was possible. They were amazed at the sight of Jesus Christ. For them, this was confirmation and evidence that the Shroud was indeed real.

Look this up on the internet, "The Shroud of Turin and The Sudarium of Oviedo." The shroud is located in Turin, Italy, and the Sudarium is located in Oviedo, Spain. It will shock you if you have never seen this before. Many believe these were the linens that covered Christ and are evidence that Christ did rise from the dead. For almost fifty years scientists have studied the cloths, but they have no explanation as to how the image became embedded in the shroud, in a three-dimensional manner. They have no idea how or why the detailed image is only visible in a photographic negative and the detail cannot be seen directly by the human eye. Remember man may not see God directly, but only in another form. Scientists have not been able to duplicate this. It is one of God's greatest mysteries. Refer to my references at the end of this book for more information.

Did someone take these burial cloths and hide them so they would not be destroyed? The fact is someone took them. They would not have left them on the floor in the cave. What if James took one cloth to Spain and John took one to Italy to keep them safe. It makes sense to split them up. It is believed these disciples had traveled to these remote locations preaching the Good News during their lifetimes.

More than likely the Mother of Jesus is the person who would have claimed these items. But remember she was being taken care of by John, the beloved one. They moved to the city of Ephesus possibly taking the cloths with them. Maybe, after Mary died they moved them for safekeeping. Possibly John, who had traveled to Rome, which is now Italy took the Shroud there. James (brother of John) became the first Church Bishop in Spain. Possibly he took the Sudarium there for safe keeping. We will never know because whatever happened to the Shroud and Sudarium was kept a secret. Certain forces wanted to destroy these items so there would be no evidence or proof of the resurrection.

There is more to the story of Joseph from Arimathea than we know from the Bible. In my references, there is one story advising who Joseph really was and what he did based on ancient writings. Joseph's life story advises he traveled to many countries during his lifetime, so he no doubt went to Italy and Spain.

There are many stories discussing how the Shroud and Sudarium came to be located where they are today. One story is that Helena the mother of Constantine found the cloths and gave them to the church. She is responsible for building the Church of the Holy Sepulchre, which now covers the tomb. The real story may never be known.

Is it possible that God provided these Holy items as evidence of the resurrection of Jesus? Perhaps God wanted us to have them, to see what Jesus actually looked like as a man. Now 2,000 years later, we can see our Lord as our ancient ancestors saw him. Was this done on purpose by God? Was this done to help intensify our faith in Christ? God works in mysterious and sometimes surprising ways. He alone controls everything in his Kingdom.

Review the facts and read about the Shroud and the Sudarium. Look at the picture of Jesus with your own eyes and then you can decide if these artifacts are real or fake. The question is, are these relics actual evidence of the resurrection of Jesus? Only you can decide.

CHAPTER 7

WHO WROTE THE NEW TESTAMENT?

W ho wrote the New Testament? There is still much debate about this subject within the Christian community. To tell the truth, only God knows who wrote the original Scriptures per His instructions. The following is a summary of which disciples are commonly accepted as the original authors of the New Testament Scriptures.

It is a confusing subject, and it's not whom you may think. One would assume that the original twelve disciples wrote the New Testament. This is not entirely correct. Only three of the original twelve disciples selected by Jesus are believed to have contributed to the New Testament writings. They were Matthew, John (son of Thunder), and Simon Peter. Matthew wrote one book. John wrote five of the books, including the Book of Revelation. Simon Peter wrote two of the books. That is a total of only eight books. There are twenty-seven approved books in the New Testament. So, who wrote the other nineteen books?

Before we find out, who wrote the other books, let's define the difference between an apostle and a disciple. The difference is a little complex, but easy to understand. To sum it up, every apostle was a disciple, but not every disciple was an apostle. Every person who believes in Jesus is called his disciple.

Matthew 28:19-20 (WEB), *Jesus came to them and spoke to them, saying, "All authority has been given to me in heaven and on earth. Go, and make disciples of all nations, baptizing them in the name of the Father and of the Son and of the Holy Spirit, teaching them to observe all things that I commanded you. Behold, I am with you always, even to the end of the age." Amen.*

The word "disciple" means "learner or student." It is used to refer to people who believed in Jesus. The Greek word "apostle" literally means "one who is sent." It can refer to an emissary or someone sent on a mission. An apostle is given authority by the one who sent him. All of the apostles were also disciples.

The twelve apostles are also frequently called the "disciples." The word apostle defines a person in terms of their mission. The term disciple emphasizes the person's relationship with the teacher. In the case of the twelve apostles, all of them are disciples. They started as disciples and ended up being apostles when they went out to teach the news of Jesus.

There were other disciples who were appointed by the original twelve, and then they would appoint another person … and so on. Slowly they increased their numbers to include disciples, apostles, teachers, evangelists, and church leaders. There is a long list of people who came to Christ within a few short years after He rose to God.

Moving ahead, others who wrote books used in the New Testament were also disciples or apostles, but they were not of the original Twelve. They were Paul (Timothy assisted Paul in writing four of the books), Jude, Luke, James, and Mark. So, this adds up to a grand total of eight people who are accredited with writing the New Testament.

Of these, Paul was the only one who was commanded directly by Jesus to spread the word to the Gentiles. Paul was a prolific writer and wrote fourteen of the books. His faith and belief were super-strong. Jude, James, and Mark each wrote one book. Luke wrote two books, Acts, and Luke.

It is generally accepted that the New Testament is made up of twenty-seven approved books. There are other books, but they are not recognized by most churches or the Council of Churches. The New Testament starts with the Book of Matthew and ends with the Book of Revelation. The first four books Matthew, Mark, Luke, and John, are commonly known as the Synoptic Gospels. These books report what these four men witnessed and/or were told about the acts of Jesus and his teachings. The most complete and detailed one is the Book of Matthew.

Jesus did not write any of the New Testament. His life and miracles were written and acknowledged mostly in the Gospels and the other books of the New

Testament. Each disciple, Matthew, Mark, Luke, and John provide similar but different stories while stressing various areas of importance as to what Christ did here on earth.

It should be noted that Peter, Matthew, and John were apostles who personally knew Jesus and were part of the original twelve. Luke and Mark were loyal disciples but had never met Jesus. Luke worked with Paul and received information about Jesus from him. It is interesting that Luke was not Jewish. Paul also did not know Christ in person, but Jesus spoke to him from above. Paul probably obtained much of his information from the original twelve. Mark was an associate of Peter and recorded what Peter had advised him about Jesus.

The Gospel of Matthew, as I mentioned, is the most detailed, and that is why it's the first book in the New Testament. Who was Matthew? He was one of Christ's original disciples and was at one time a tax collector in the village of Capernaum. His given name was Levi, but Jesus changed it to Matthew. Since he was a tax collector he paid a lot of attention to details, and one would surmise that is why his Gospel is the most detailed book about Christ. In ancient times tax collectors were despised by everyone, so Matthew had few, if any close friends until he met Jesus. He was well off compared to others in his little village, but he gave up everything to follow Christ.

Capernaum was built along the edge of the Sea of Galilee and probably had about fifteen hundred residents. It was a sleepy fishing village. Peter, Andrew,

James, and John were fishermen who also lived in the village. A total of four disciples came from this little village who were fishermen. These men most likely knew each other and were probably already friends with similar beliefs. The Bible doesn't go into great detail about lives of these men.

Simon Peter (son of Jonah) was the rock with which Christ would build His Church. The name Peter actually means "rock."

Matthew 16:16-19 (WEB), *Simon Peter answered, "You are the Christ, the Son of the living God."*

Jesus answered him, "Blessed are you, Simon Bar Jonah, for flesh and blood has not revealed this to you, but my Father who is in heaven. I also tell you that you are Peter, and on this rock, I will build my assembly, and the gates of Hades will not prevail against it. I will give to you the keys of the Kingdom of Heaven, and whatever you bind on earth will have been bound in heaven; and whatever you release on earth will have been released in heaven."

Now here is the interesting part. James and John were brothers. Peter and Andrew were brothers. As mentioned these four men were fishermen and had to know each other in the little village of Capernaum. It should be noted that Andrew was a disciple of John the Baptist before meeting Jesus.

Another interesting fact is that Matthew, the tax collector, and James (son of Alphaeus) were most likely brothers. Both were sons of Alphaeus, according to ancient writings.

We have three sets of brothers who were all from the same village or area. Four of them were fishermen. They were actually partners in the fishing business. We have a total of six disciples from Capernaum out of the original twelve. Now we know why this little village was important.

Capernaum was one of the three cities cursed by Jesus for its lack of faith and inclination towards sin, therefore, Jesus decided to start here. The center of the Jesus ministry was an area now called the "evangelical triangle." The small towns of Capernaum, Bethsaida, and Chorazin were located on the points of the triangle. All three cities showed little faith in God.

One more point of interest is that two disciples, Simon (the Zealot) and Bartholomew (Nathanael), came from the little town Cana, which is not far from Capernaum. Philip was from Bethsaida, one of the three triangle points. Thomas and Thaddaeus lived somewhere nearby in the Galilee area. Therefore, it can be concluded that eleven of the twelve disciples came from the sea of Galilee area.

Judas, who betrayed Jesus, was the only one from outside of the area. He originally lived in the village of Kerioth, which is south of Jerusalem, near Hebron. Kerioth is located far from the land of Galilee. So that made him an outsider from the start and possibly he had trouble fitting in with the group.

In a small fishing village, everyone certainly knew

everyone else living there. The Word of Jesus could spread fast if he selected the right people. It is not known how religious these men were before they met Jesus, but they apparently thirsted for God. They accepted the calling of Christ.

In Capernaum, Jesus healed the servant of the centurion: **Luke 7:3 (WEB)**, *When he heard about Jesus, he sent to him elders of the Jews, asking him to come and save his servant.*

This Roman centurion was a powerful person, but he saw the good Jesus was doing and how he ministered to the people. He had strong faith in Christ. This official was credited with building the Capernaum synagogue even though he wasn't Jewish. But he had the strongest faith in Jesus Christ.

Centurions were the commanders or captains of a one-hundred-man unit. It is said they were the bravest and best fighters in the Roman army. The centurions would handle any local disputes and maintain law and order. Most centurions were feared by the people they ruled over.

In Capernaum, Jesus gave a sermon on the "**Bread of Life**." Refer to **John 6:25-59** for the full sermon.

John 6:35-40 (KJV), *And Jesus said unto them, I am the bread of life: he that cometh to me shall never hunger; and he that believeth on me shall never thirst.*

But I said unto you, that ye also have seen me, and believe not.

All that the Father giveth me shall come to me; and

him that cometh to me I will in no wise cast out.

For I came down from heaven, not to do mine own will, but the will of him that sent me.

And this is the Father's will which hath sent me, that of all which he hath given me I should lose nothing, but should raise it up again at the last day.

And this is the will of him that sent me, that every one which seeth the Son, and believeth on him, may have everlasting life: and I will raise him up at the last day.

In this sermon, Jesus was telling the people exactly who he was. Jesus talks about being the bread of life and drinking His blood. He says, *"I am the bread of life."* This is very similar to the Last Supper when he breaks bread with his disciples, and they drink from the cup, a symbol of his blood.

It can be concluded that not all of the men who wrote the New Testament were part of the original twelve disciples. The twelve disciples were: Peter, James (son of Zebedee), John, Andrew, Philip, Bartholomew (Nathanael), Matthew, Thomas, James (son of Alphaeus), Thaddaeus, Simon (the Zealot), and Judas (the Betrayer).

The authors of the New Testament, according to our best information, were: Matthew, Mark, Luke, John, Paul, James (brother of Jesus), Peter, and Jude (brother of Jesus). A total of eight men contributed to the Good News.

Who were these men? What were they like? What

happened to all the disciples? Did they just fade into history? Before discussing that, there is one more book not in the New Testament that should be mentioned because it was written by Thomas, one of the original twelve.

There are many books that were found written about Christ, but not all were selected to be put in the New Testament for various reasons, unknown to most of us. One of these is the Gospel of Thomas. Yes, Doubting Thomas, who had to stick his hand into the wounds of Jesus to believe it was he who came back to life. The complete version, written in Coptic, suggests that it was probably composed in Greek first, or Aramaic, in the mid-first century. The Gospel of Thomas has no stories in the scripture form. It is simply a list of 114 sayings of Jesus, according to Thomas, that are deemed important. They are in no particular order. Here are the first two examples from Thomas.

Gospel of Thomas, *"These are the secret sayings which the living Jesus spoke and which Thomas wrote down."*

1) *And Jesus said, "Whoever finds the interpretation of these sayings will not experience death."*

2) *Jesus said, "Let him who seeks continue seeking until he finds. When he finds, he will become troubled. When he becomes troubled, he will be astonished, and he will rule over the All."*

Reading the sayings of Jesus, as written by Thomas, is interesting. If you want to read more of them you can find the Book of Thomas, in English, on the internet.

Read the next chapter to find out more about the twelve disciples and the amazing men who wrote the New Testament. Find out more about the incredible women disciples who served Christ in life and after he had risen to the Father. They provided the necessary support and supplies for the disciples. They had unbelievable faith in God and His Son Jesus Christ.

CHAPTER 8

WHO WERE THE DISCIPLES, and WHAT HAPPENED TO THEM?

Mark 3:13-15 (WEB), He *went up into the mountain, and called to himself those whom he wanted, and they went to him. He appointed twelve, that they might be with him, and that he might send them out to preach, and to have authority to heal sicknesses and to cast out demons.*

Jesus only appointed twelve disciples; however, there were actually many more than twelve. No one knows how many for sure, but in my research, I found fifty-one names of people all mentioned in the New Testament. Scripture states that when the Holy Spirit came one hundred-twenty disciples were present.

We don't know a lot about the disciples. The disciples were amazing people who traveled the known world at the time teaching about Jesus and the New Covenant. They were brave men and women who knew preaching the Words of Jesus could mean death. Who were these men and women who followed Jesus and died for their beliefs? Continue reading to find out why they are important figures in the New Testament.

Mark 6:7-9 (WEB), He *called to Himself the twelve, and began to send them out two by two, and he gave them authority over the unclean spirits. He commanded them that they should take nothing for their journey, except a staff only: no bread, no wallet, no money in their purse, but to wear sandals, and not put on two tunics.*

The **Book of Acts** gives an accounting of what many disciples and apostles did, and where they went to preach the words of Christ. It also tells of the good deeds and miracles they performed.

Acts 5:12-16 (WEB), *By the hands of the apostle's many signs and wonders were done among the people. They were all with one accord in Solomon's porch. None of the rest dared to join them, however, the people honored them. More believers were added to the Lord, multitudes of both men and women. They even carried out the sick into the streets, and laid them on cots and mattresses, so that as Peter came by, at the least his shadow might overshadow some of them. Multitudes also came together from the cities around Jerusalem, bringing sick people, and those who were tormented by unclean spirits: and they were all healed.*

After Jesus ascended, the disciples were all waiting in Jerusalem for the Holy Spirit to come, as Jesus said it would, to baptize them. He told them, "*You will receive power when the Holy Spirit comes on you and you will be my witnesses to the ends of the earth.*"

On the morning of the Pentecost, one hundred-twenty disciples received the Holy Spirit as Jesus had advised them.

Acts 2:1-4 (WEB), *Now when the day of Pentecost had come, they were all with one accord in one place. Suddenly there came from the sky a sound like the rushing of a mighty wind, and it filled all the house where they were sitting. Tongues like fire appeared and were distributed to them, and one sat on each of them. They were all filled with the Holy Spirit and began to speak with other languages, as the Spirit gave them the ability to speak.*

Now the disciples had the ability to speak different languages and to perform miracles preaching about the New Covenant and Jesus Christ all over the known world without fear. They didn't fear what would happen to them, and they didn't worry about it, for they knew God was with them forever. These men and women had seen and experienced the wondrous works of God. They had powerful faith that no matter what happened they could trust in the Lord.

Note: The Feast of Pentecost, which gives thanks to God for a harvest, is celebrated fifty days after Passover, thereby the name. It is also the occasion when Moses received the Ten Commandments from God.

As already mentioned the twelve original disciples were: Peter, James (son of Zebedee), John (son of Zebedee), Andrew, Philip, Bartholomew (Nathanael), Matthew, Thomas, James (son of Alphaeus), Thaddaeus, Simon (the Zealot), and Judas (the Betrayer). Judas was replaced by Matthias.

The eight major authors of the New Testament, according to our best information, were: Matthew, Mark, Luke, John, Paul, James (brother of Jesus), Peter, and Jude (brother of Jesus).

We will review what happened to the original twelve disciples and also to Mark, Luke, James, Jude, and Paul (the five) who were not part of the original twelve, but helped write the New Testament. The information about them is taken from the New Testament and from ancient writings.

The Bible reports the deaths of only two disciples; Judas, who hung himself, and James (son of Zebedee), who was executed by the sword. Most of the original twelve disciples suffered terrible deaths for their preaching of the Good News, according to ancient records.

The twelve key disciples started the Christian movement, along with the "Five" and help from many others. These people were the ones that Jesus knew would carry forward the idea of a New Covenant. However, without the Five (Mark, Luke, James, Jude, and Paul), the New Testament would not have been as complete. We are blessed that two thousand years later we can read their Holy Words inspired by God. God was pushing their minds, hearts, and hands as they wrote the Good News.

THE TWELVE

Peter or Simon Peter, Known as the Rock

He was a fisherman from Bethsaida, but lived in Capernaum along with his brother Andrew, as already stated. It is reported that he was married and became one of the pillars of the Jerusalem church. Peter wrote two of the books in the New Testament (Peter 1 and 2).

He was part of the inner circle, along with James and John (sons of Thunder), who were witness to the Transfiguration of Jesus, when his divinity was revealed. Only these three disciples witnessed the spirit of Moses, Elijah, and the Cloud of God, which descended from heaven to meet Christ.

Peter was hot-tempered and protective of Jesus, as detailed in **John 18:4-10, (WEB)**, *Jesus therefore, knowing all the things that were happening to him, went out, and said to them, "Who are you looking for?"*

They answered him, "Jesus of Nazareth."

Jesus said to them, "I am he."

Judas also, who betrayed him, was standing with them. When therefore he said to them, "I am He," they went backward, and fell to the ground.

Again, therefore, he asked them, "Who are you looking for?"

They said, "Jesus of Nazareth."

Jesus answered, "I told you that I am he. If therefore you seek me, let these go their way," that the word might be fulfilled which he spoke, "Of those whom you have given me, I have lost none."

Simon Peter, therefore, having a sword, drew it, and struck the high priest's servant, and cut off his right ear. The servant's name was Malchus.

Surprisingly Peter cuts the ear off of Malchus, showing his anger and desire to protect Jesus. At a later date, after the Pentecost, Peter was put in jail by Herod for preaching and probably would have been killed, but he was released by an angel of the Lord. He escaped certain death at the hands of Herod.

Peter ministered to Jews and Gentiles after the Pentecost. He was the rock or foundation for the new Church of Christ. The name Peter (Cephas) means "Rock." Jesus told him, as stated in **Matthew 16:18 (KJV)**, *"And I say also unto thee, that thou art Peter, and upon this rock I will build my church; and the gates of hell shall not prevail against it."*

It is said and possibly recorded somewhere in Roman history, that Peter was crucified upside down during the reign of Nero in Rome.

James, Son of Zebedee

James was the older of the two apostle sons of Zebedee. Jesus nicknamed them the "sons of Thunder." It is said he was thirty years old when he became an apostle. He was married, had four children, and lived near his parents on the outskirts of Capernaum.

It was the "sons of Thunder" who wanted to call fire down from God to destroy the Samaritans who showed disrespect to Christ.

James was a fisherman along with his brother John and father. He was a pillar of the Jerusalem church. His ministry was wide-spread, and it is rumored that James became the first bishop of Spain. This is a debatable subject in many circles because there is no record of James traveling there. But no one knows for sure. According to Spanish information, his body was taken to Santiago de Compostela, where today his shrine attracts thousands of pilgrims from all over the world.

James died a violent death at the hands of Herod Agrippa I. He is the only disciple whose death, by a sword, was recorded in the scripture.

Acts 12:1-2 (WEB), *Now about that time, King Herod stretched out his hands to oppress some of the assembly. He killed James, the brother of John, with the sword.*

John, Son of Zebedee

John was the beloved disciple of Jesus. John was the brother of James. He also was a pillar of the Jerusalem church. He healed the sick and preached. John wrote five books: John, John 1 through 3, and Revelation. It is assumed that John was the one responsible for taking care of Mary, the mother of Jesus.

John was somewhat vengeful and fiery as was his brother James as stated in **Luke**.

Luke 9:51-56 (WEB), *It came to pass, when the days were near that he should be taken up, he intently set his face to go to Jerusalem, and sent messengers before Him. They went, and entered into a village of the Samaritans, so as to prepare for Him. They did not receive him, because he was traveling with his face set towards Jerusalem. When His disciples, James and John, saw this, they said, "Lord, do you want us to command fire to come down from the sky, and destroy them, just as Elijah did?"*

But he turned and rebuked them, "You don't know what kind of spirit you are. For the Son of Man didn't come to destroy men's lives, but to save them."

So, they went to another village.

I was clear that John and James wanted to teach the Samaritans a lesson. They were not pleased that the Samaritan village didn't accept the visit of Jesus.

John was arrested and exiled to an island named Patmos for his teachings by the Roman authorities. It was at Patmos that he received instructions from Christ to write everything that he had witnessed, what was, what is now, and what will take place in the future. At this time there were seven major churches located in the ancient world: Ephesus, Smyrna, Pergamum, Thyatira, Sardis, Philadelphia, and Laodicea. John wrote to each church advising what he had been told to do.

Some stories suggest that John was released from Patmos, and went back to the church in Ephesus, which is located in modern-day Turkey. There he died a natural death in AD 100.

Andrew, the First Called

The name Andrew means "manly." Andrew was born in Bethsaida, but he lived in Capernaum along with Simon Peter, his brother. He was also a fisherman. Andrew was a disciple of John the Baptist before meeting Jesus. This made him one of the first to be called.

John 1:41-42 (WEB), *One of the two who heard John, and followed him, was Andrew, Simon Peter's brother. He first found his own brother, Simon, and said to him, "We have found the Messiah!" (which is, being interpreted, Christ).*

He brought him to Jesus. Jesus looked at him, and said, "You are Simon the son of Jonah. You shall be called Cephas" (which by interpretation is Peter).

Andrew was very enthusiastic about Christ and set out to preach to the Jews, heal the sick, cleanse the lepers, cast out demons, and raise the dead when it seemed a proper thing to do.

Andrew ended up preaching in Asia Minor, Greece, and Russia teaching the Words of Christ. Records state that he was crucified on an X shaped cross by a Roman official.

Philip

Philip was born in Bethsaida, as stated in **John 1:44**, and was one of the Twelve. He probably spoke Greek, since his name is Greek based. He was the third disciple called to serve. It is said that he lived and preached in

Scythia most of the time, which is located in modern-day Ukraine. His name in Greek means "one who loves horses."

John 1:44 (WEB), *Now Philip was from Bethsaida, of the city of Andrew and Peter. Philip found Nathanael, and said to him, "We have found him, of whom Moses in the law, and the prophets wrote: Jesus of Nazareth, the son of Joseph."*

Philip asked Jesus to show him the Father: **John 14:8-10 (WEB)**, *Philip said to him, "Lord, show us the Father, and that will be enough for us."*

Jesus said to him, "Have I been with you such a long time, and do you not know me, Philip? He who has seen me has seen the Father. How do you say, 'Show us the Father?' Don't you believe that I am in the Father and the Father in me? The words that I tell you, I speak not from myself; but the Father who lives in me does His works."

Philip was very practical and helpful when it came to gaining new believers. **John 12:20-22 (WEB)**, *Now there were certain Greeks among those that went up to worship at the feast. These, therefore, came to Philip, who was from Bethsaida of Galilee, and asked him, saying, "Sir, we want to see Jesus." Philip came and told Andrew, and in turn, Andrew came with Philip, and they told Jesus.*

Some stories suggest that Philip was crucified on a tall cross in Hierapolis of Phrygia, which would be in Turkey today.

Bartholomew (Nathanael)

By all accounts, Bartholomew was born and raised in the area of Galilee. He was usually called Nathanael in the Bible and was well versed in the Hebrew Scriptures. "Bartholomew" is Greek for "son of Tolmai," while "Nathanael" is a Hebrew name and means "God has given."

The following conversation gives you some idea of who Nathanael was.

John 1:46-51 (WEB), *Nathanael said to him, "Can any good thing come out of Nazareth?"*

Philip said to him, "Come and see."

Jesus saw Nathanael coming to him, and said about him, "Behold, an Israelite indeed, in whom is no deceit!"

Nathanael said to him, "How do you know me?"

Jesus answered him, "Before Philip called you, when you were under the fig tree, I saw you."

Nathanael answered him, "Rabbi, you are the Son of God! You are King of Israel!"

Jesus answered him, "Because I told you, 'I saw you underneath the fig tree,' do you believe? You will see greater things than these!" He said to him, "Most certainly, I tell you, hereafter you will see heaven opened, and the angels of God ascending and descending on the Son of Man."

Nathanael is said to have ministered in Asia Minor

and India. The Armenian Church claims Bartholomew (Nathanael) as their founder. Because of his teachings, he was skinned alive in Armenia according to ancient records.

Matthew or Levi, Son of Alphaeus

He was from Capernaum, as was his brother James (son of Alphaeus). Matthew wrote the Book of Matthew, the first book in the New Testament. His name means "gift of God." he had to be a very detailed man when it came to keeping records because he was a tax collector for Rome.

When Jesus met Matthew, he was sitting at a tax collectors' booth. Matthew followed Jesus, and later he had Jesus visit his home to have dinner.

Matthew 9:10-13 (WEB), *As he sat in the house, behold, many tax collectors and sinners came and sat down with Jesus and his disciples. When the Pharisees saw it, they said to his disciples, "Why does your teacher eat with tax collectors and sinners?"*

When Jesus heard it, he said to them, "Those who are healthy have no need for a physician, but those who are sick do. But you go and learn what this means: 'I desire mercy, and not sacrifice,' for I came not to call the righteous, but sinners to repentance."

Jesus sent Matthew out to preach, as stated in **Matthew 10:6-8 (WEB)**, *"Rather, go to the lost sheep of the house of Israel. As you go, preach, saying, 'The Kingdom of Heaven is at hand!' Heal the sick, cleanse* *the lepers, and cast out demons. Freely you received, so freely give."*

He ministered to Israel, Persia, Macedonia, Syria, and Ethiopia. It is not fully known how he died, but stories suggest he had a violent death. Matthew was martyred with an ax or sword in Ethiopia according to one story.

Thomas or Doubting Thomas

He was listed as one of the original twelve that was called by Jesus. Refer to **Matthew 10:2-4 (WEB)**, *Now the names of the twelve apostles are these. The first, Simon, who is called Peter; Andrew, his brother; James the son of Zebedee; John, his brother; Philip; Bartholomew; Thomas; Matthew the tax collector; James the son of Alphaeus; Lebbaeus, who was also called Thaddaeus; Simon the Canaanite; and Judas Iscariot, who also betrayed him.*

Thomas doubted that Jesus was resurrected saying he needed to touch His wounds in order to believe.

John 20:24-28 (WEB), *But Thomas, one of the twelve, called Didymus, wasn't with them when Jesus came. The other disciples, therefore, said to him, "We have seen the Lord!"*

But he said to them, "Unless I see in his hands the print of the nails, and put my hand into his side, I will not believe."

After eight days again his disciples were inside, and

117

Thomas was with them. Jesus came, the doors being locked, and stood in the middle, and said, "Peace be to you." Then he said to Thomas, "Reach here your finger and see my hands. Reach here your hand, and put it into my side. Don't be unbelieving, but believing."

Thomas answered him, "My Lord and my God!"

Thomas wrote the Gospel of Thomas which is one hundred fourteen sayings of Jesus. It is not included in today's New Testament. It is suggested that Thomas traveled to India and founded the Christian church there. He was killed by a spear for his faith and buried there, but the exact location isn't known.

James, Son of Alphaeus

James was the son of Alphaeus and a possible brother to Matthew. He is often confused with James (the brother of Jesus), or James, son of Zebedee. Being one of the Twelve he was at the Last Supper as were the others. James was present when Jesus appeared to the disciples after the resurrection.

Some believe he belonged to a revolutionary group known as the Zealots. The Zealots were a political movement in the first century in Israel. They sought to incite the people of Judaea Province to rebel against the Roman Empire. The Zealots turned into a violent group by AD 66 and started the first Jewish–Roman War (AD 66–70). The capital, Jerusalem, was destroyed by the Romans in AD 70.

It is thought that James was crucified in the Sinai or

in Persia, but some believe he was stoned to death in Jerusalem by the Jews.

Thaddaeus or Judas, Son of James

His name means "beloved." He was listed as one of the Twelve in **Matthew 10:2-4**. He is not to be confused with Jude, the brother of Jesus, or Judas, the disciple, who betrayed Jesus. Thaddaeus asked Jesus why he reveals himself to his followers, and not to the world.

John 14:22-24 (WEB), *Judas (not Iscariot) said to him, "Lord, what has happened that you are about to reveal yourself to us, and not to the world?"*

Jesus answered him, "If a man loves me, he will keep my word. My Father will love him, and we will come to him, and make our home with him. He who does not love me does not keep my words. The word which you hear isn't mine, but the Father's who sent me."

It is believed that Thaddaeus was also in the revolutionary group the Zealots, as were a few other disciples. Little is known about Thaddaeus, the apostle with four names in the Bible. Most scholars agree, however, that the four names used for him all refer to the same person.

In lists of the Twelve, he is called Thaddeus or Thaddaeus, a surname for the name Lebbaeus as mentioned in **Matthew 10:3.** It means "courageous heart." The picture is blurred when he is called Judas, not the same man as Judas Iscariot.

More confusion is caused when he is called Jude. Some Bible scholars believe Thaddeus wrote the book of Jude. Most take the view that Jude, the brother of Jesus, is the author. This is easily proven by referring to **Jude 1-2 (WEB)**, *"Jude, a servant of Jesus Christ, and brother of James, to those who are called."*

Thaddeus had no brother named James which proves he did not write the Book of Jude. Thaddeus did have a father named James. Christ's two brothers were James and Jude who authored the books in their names.

Church tradition states that Thaddeus founded the church in Edessa and was killed there as a martyr. However, it is also written in ancient texts that while preaching in Iran he was hacked to death along with Simon the Zealot.

Simon the Zealot

Simon is also called Simon the Cananaean (meaning "zealous one"). He was of the Twelve and had the same missions as the others. He is possibly the brother of Nathanael, but this is only speculation.

Simon was the eleventh apostle chosen by Christ. Research says he was a man of good ancestry and lived with his family in Capernaum. He was 28 years old when he became a disciple. It is believed he was an agitator who spoke without thinking. It is written that before becoming a disciple he was a merchant. What he sold isn't known.

Simon was a Zealot because he was against taxes,

as was James (son of Alphaeus). He went to teach the Good News in Persia, which today is Iran. There he was murdered with Thaddaeus, according to one story. In another, he traveled into deep dark Africa and died there.

Judas the Betrayer

We all know what Judas did, so we won't discuss that. Judas was the treasurer for the disciples and also was a thief.

John 12:4-6 (WEB), *Then Judas Iscariot, Simon's son, one of His disciples, who would betray Him, said, "Why wasn't this ointment sold for three hundred denarii, and given to the poor?"*

Now he said this, not because he cared for the poor, but because he was a thief, and having the money box, used to steal what was put into it.

Based on the above, we can assume that John didn't like Judas, calling him a thief. Judas was of bad character. There was nothing good about him. Jesus knew that but made him a disciple for a reason. The reason was to fulfill God's plan.

John 13:1-3 (WEB), *Now before the feast of the Passover, Jesus, knowing that his time had come that he would depart from this world to the Father, having loved his own who were in the world, he loved them to the end. During supper, the devil having already put into the heart of Judas Iscariot, Simon's son, to betray him, Jesus, knowing that the Father had given all things into* *his hands, and that he came from God, and was going to God, ...*

It is commonly accepted that Judas hung himself as stated in the Bible.

Comments

The above people were the original Twelve disciples. As you can see, not much is known about them, and most died for spreading the Good News around the known world at the time.

As already mentioned eight disciples wrote the New Testament who were: Matthew, Mark, Luke, John, Paul, James, Peter, and Jude. Three are of the original Twelve, and Five are not of the Twelve.

THE FIVE (Who Helped Write the New Testament)

Other disciples, not of the Twelve, that deserve mention since they wrote most of the New Testament are Mark, Luke, Paul, James, and Jude, whom I designate as "**The Five.**"

Mark (John Mark)

Mark may have been younger than other writers of the New Testament. His mother was a prominent follower of Jesus Christ. **Acts 12:12** tells us that her name was Mary, the mother of Mark. Some believe that her house in Jerusalem was used as a meeting place for the disciples. From the scripture verse, we also find out his full name is John Mark.

The meeting place of the disciples was called the Cenacle in some records and was reportedly owned by the mother of John Mark. The Cenacle is said to be the meeting place where the Last Supper was held, the resurrection appearance of Christ to all the apostles happened, and the location that the Holy Ghost came on Pentecost.

After the resurrection, Mark first traveled with the apostle Paul. Later he accompanied Peter to Rome and stayed near him while he was in prison. Mark is known as Peter's interpreter and scribe. In his book, Mark wrote down the observations and memories of Peter, one of the original apostles. Mark's book reflects Peter's desire to spread the Gospel to the Gentiles.

Mark was Peter's scribe and wrote the Gospel of Mark based on Peter's testimony. Mark was also the cousin of Barnabas, the apostle. After serving in Rome, Mark made his way to Alexandria, where he became the first bishop. To this day, the patriarch of the Alexandria Coptic Church is Saint Mark.

One day, after returning to Alexandria from a trip, Mark found that non-believers resented his efforts to turn people away from the worship of the original Egyptian gods. It was in AD 68 they dragged him through the streets until he was dead. His relics, whatever they are, were transferred to Venice, where they are held to this day.

Luke, the Physician

It is noted that Luke was a companion of Paul, and was a trained physician. Luke wrote two books used in the New Testament. He composed the third gospel, and the Book of Acts, which is about the expansion of Christianity and works of the disciples, after the death of Jesus.

Many scholars believe Luke was a Greek physician who lived at one time in the Greek city of Antioch, which is now in Syria. Scripture historians place Luke in the company of Paul in the city of Troas around the year AD 51. He traveled with Paul throughout Macedonia to the cities of Neapolis, Samothrace, and Philippi. When Paul was imprisoned Luke stayed in Macedonia to teach the message of Jesus to encourage the Macedonian people to become believers.

Antioch, located in Syria, was the third largest city in the Roman Empire at the time. It became the capital of Syria with a population estimated to be around five hundred thousand people. Many Jews lived there, but mostly the population was Greek. Antioch was founded by Seleucus who was a general under Alexander the Great. He named the city after his son Antiochus. The church in Antioch became a large important group of people, which consisted of both Jews and Gentiles.

When Paul was released from prison in AD 58, Luke joined him and they again traveled together spreading the message of Christ. They preached in Rome, where Paul was again imprisoned, in the year AD

61. Luke was the only companion of Paul to remain at his side. Most of the information in Luke's Gospel came from his conversations with Paul. His Gospel is mostly concerned with poverty and social issues. It also mentions six miracles that seemed to be of importance to Luke.

Some suggest that Luke settled in Greece, wrote his Gospel, and died there peacefully at the age of 84. It is also rumored that individuals reported him to the Roman Emperor Nero for teaching about God. Nero sent for Luke, so he hid his writings with a trusted friend before going in front of Nero.

Nero reportedly cut off Luke's right hand. Luke performed a miracle by reattaching it to this body. This greatly upset the emperor, and he responded by cutting off Luke's head and ordered his body be thrown into the sea. Nero was not going to be outdone by a Christian disciple.

Luke showed no fear because of his faith in Christ.

James, Brother of Jesus

As discussed earlier, James was present with the apostles in Jerusalem when the church began, after Christ rose to God as noted in **Acts 1:14**. James later became the leader of the church in Jerusalem. He is the author of the New Testament book in his name.

As a leader in Jerusalem, James spoke out against circumcision of Gentile believers as mentioned in **Acts 15:1-2 (WEB)**, *Some men came down from Judea and* *taught the brothers, "Unless you are circumcised after the custom of Moses, you can't be saved." Therefore Paul and Barnabas had a sharp dispute and debate with them. So they appointed Paul and Barnabas, and some others of them, to go up to Jerusalem to see the apostles and elders about this question.*

James, Paul, and Barnabas did not want to force Gentiles to be circumcised because they knew that would make a problem for the acceptance of Christ. After much debate, it was finally agreed that Gentiles wouldn't need to follow the ancient Jewish law in this matter.

According to the first-century Jewish historian Josephus, the Jewish religious hierarchy stoned and killed James, *"the brother of Jesus, who was called Christ, whose name was James"* (***Antiquities of the Jews* 20.200**). The year was about AD 62.

Matthew and Mark recorded an incident mentioning James' name, where his fellow townsmen made fun of Jesus, seeing him as nothing special, but merely a local.

Matthew 13:55-56 (WEB), *"Isn't this the carpenter's son? Isn't His mother called Mary, and His brothers, James, Joses, Simon, and Judas? Aren't all of His sisters with us? Where then did this man get all of these things?"*

In earlier times James and the rest of the family were opposed to Jesus' ministry and teaching.

John 7:5 (WEB) tells us, *"For even his brothers didn't believe in him."*

However, James and his brothers all came to be believers. James soon became the leader of the Jerusalem church. Paul met with him and Peter when he first went to Jerusalem as stated in **Galatians 1:18–19 (WEB),** *Then after three years I went up to Jerusalem to visit Peter and stayed with him fifteen days. But of the other apostles, I saw no one, except James, the Lord's brother.*

Paul met James on another occasion when he brought famine relief to Jerusalem from other churches outside Judea, which is stated in **Acts 21:17-19 (WEB),** *When we had come to Jerusalem, the brothers received us gladly. The day following, Paul went in with us to James; and all the elders were present. When he had greeted them, he reported one by one the things which God had worked among the Gentiles through his ministry.*

An ancient church historian, named Eusebius, noted that Peter and John chose James to lead the church in Jerusalem. Historical writing in the fifth century, says that James *"ruled the Church of Jerusalem thirty years, until the seventh year of Nero."*

The second-century historian Hegesippus wrote; *"following James's death the Church chose another of Jesus' blood relatives, his cousin Simon, to be leader of the Jerusalem church."*

The statement, *"chose another of Jesus' blood relatives,"* means that James was the faithful half-brother of Jesus.

Jude, Brother of Jesus

Jude wrote the Book of Jude. Please note that this is not the same Judas that betrayed Christ. From **Jude 1-2 (WEB)**, *Jude, a servant of Jesus Christ, and brother of James, to those who are called, sanctified by God the Father, and kept for Jesus Christ: Mercy to you and peace and love be multiplied.*

The above verse clearly states that Jude is the brother of James. Therefore, he is also the half-brother of Jesus.

After the ascension of Jesus, Jude started to travel, preaching the Gospel. His journeys took him to Judea, Galilee, Samaria, Arabia, Syria, and Mesopotamia. Finally, he went to the city of Edessa. Here he finished the work that wasn't completed by his predecessor, Thaddeus (one of the Twelve). Edessa was a city in upper Mesopotamia, founded in 302 BC. Thanks to the efforts of Jude it became an important location for Christianity, in ancient times.

Jude urged believers not to sin, be faithful, and to love one another. He also stressed to beware of false teachers. He believed that faith must be backed up by good deeds.

It is reported that Jude died as a martyr in AD 80 near Mt. Ararat in Armenia. He was crucified and/or killed by arrows. He had total faith in his half-brother Jesus the Christ.

Paul or Saul

What an amazing man Paul was. He wrote fourteen of the books or was responsible for most of them, which are now used in the New Testament. But you would never know that because not one book is named after him. Four of his books were written with the help of other disciples. He was a wonderful apostle of Christ, spreading the Words of God.

Paul was appointed by Christ after He had gone to God the Father, as stated in **Galatians 1:1 (KJV)**, *Paul, an apostle, (not of men, neither by man, but by Jesus Christ, and God the Father, who raised him from the dead).*

The commonly accepted that the following books are from Paul: Romans, Corinthians 1 and 2, Galatians, Ephesians, Philippians, Colossians, Thessalonians 1 and 2, Timothy 1 and 2, Titus, Philemon, and Hebrews.

Not only did he become an amazing author and disciple, but he was also a tough guy. He was a man unafraid to fight and stand up for what he believed. Maybe this is why Jesus chose him.

Paul was a Jew, born in the Roman city of Tarsus. He was a Roman citizen, but was proud of his Jewish heritage, as he describes in **Acts 22:1-5 (WEB)**, *"Brothers and fathers, listen to the defense which I now make to you."*

When they heard that he spoke to them in the Hebrew language, they were even quieter. He said, "I am indeed a Jew, born in Tarsus of Cilicia, but brought

129

up in this city at the feet of Gamaliel, instructed according to the strict tradition of the law of our fathers, being zealous for God, even as you all are today. I persecuted the Way to the death, binding and delivering into prisons both men and women. As also the high priest and all the council of the elders testify, from whom also I received letters to the brothers, and traveled to Damascus to bring them who were there to Jerusalem in bonds to be punished."

It should be noted that Gamaliel was a Jewish Pharisee, a teacher of the law, who was honored by all the Jewish people. Gamaliel taught Saul about Jewish law and he became zealous and devout persecuting Christians to show his devotion to the Jewish faith.

He chose to use his Hebrew name *Saul* until he became a believer, and started preaching about Christ. Paul was known as "the apostle to the gentiles." It made a lot of sense for Paul to use his Roman name as he traveled into the land of the Gentiles.

Saul was on his way to Damascus to hunt down Christians, or believers in the "Way," an early term used before the word Christian became common. Saul hated Christians, and any that he found would be arrested and taken back to Jerusalem for trial.

The story of Saul's conversion starts here, after Christ had risen. On the road, near Damascus, a light from heaven flashed around him knocking him to the ground.

Acts 9: 4-19 (WEB), *he fell on the earth, and heard a voice saying to him, "Saul, Saul, why do you* *persecute me?"*

He said, "Who are you, Lord?"

The Lord said, "I am Jesus, whom you are persecuting. But rise up, and enter into the city, and you will be told what you must do."

The men who traveled with him stood speechless, hearing the sound, but seeing no one. Saul arose from the ground, and when his eyes were opened, he saw no one. They led him by the hand and brought him into Damascus. He was without sight for three days, and neither ate nor drank.

Now there was a certain disciple at Damascus named Ananias. The Lord said to him in a vision, "Ananias!"

He said, "Behold, it's me, Lord."

The Lord said to him, "Arise, and go to the street which is called Straight, and inquire in the house of Judah for one named Saul, a man of Tarsus. For behold, he is praying, and in a vision he has seen a man named Ananias coming in, and laying his hands on him, that he might receive his sight."

But Ananias answered, "Lord, I have heard from many about this man, how much evil he did to your saints at Jerusalem. Here he has authority from the chief priests to bind all who call on your name."

But the Lord said to him, "Go your way, for he is my chosen vessel to bear my name before the nations and kings, and the children of Israel. For I will show him how many things he must suffer for my name's sake."

Ananias departed, and entered into the house. Laying his hands on him, he said, "Brother Saul, the Lord, who appeared to you on the road by which you came, has sent me, that you may receive your sight, and be filled with the Holy Spirit." Immediately something like scales fell from his eyes, and he received his sight. He arose and was baptized. He took food and was strengthened. Saul stayed several days with the disciples who were at Damascus.

Almost overnight the Lord Jesus made Saul a believer and a faithful disciple. At once he began preaching wherever he could. Jesus gave him faith.

The Bible doesn't tell us how the apostle Paul died. In his writing's Paul seems to be predicting his own death: **2 Timothy 4: 6-8 (WEB)**, *"For I am already being offered, and the time of my departure has come. I have fought the good fight. I have finished the course. I have kept the faith. From now on, there is stored up for me the crown of righteousness, which the Lord, the righteous judge, will give to me on that day; and not to me only, but also to all those who have loved his appearing."*

The second Book of Timothy was written during Paul's second Roman imprisonment. From the writings of an early church historian named Eusebius, he claims that Paul was beheaded at the order of the Roman emperor Nero. Paul was killed shortly after Rome had burned, which Nero blamed on Christians. It is said that

Nero actually was the one who started the fire.

During this period Christians were being persecuted by Rome, so it's also possible that the apostle Peter was killed around the same time in Rome. Because Paul was a Roman citizen they were normally exempt from being crucified.

Acts 22:28 (WEB), *The commanding officer answered, "I bought my citizenship for a great price."*

Paul said, "But I was born a Roman."

It is believed that Paul was beheaded under orders of Emperor Nero sometime in AD 68.

Paul wrote in **Galatians 6:17 (KJV)**, *From henceforth let no man trouble me: for I bear in my body the marks of the Lord Jesus.*

Paul loved the Lord Jesus and was faithful until the end of his time on earth.

THE WOMEN DISCIPLES

Women in ancient days had little say-so in the matters of religion, or for that matter, anything that was outside of the home. That all changed when Jesus came along. Christian women were empowered to become active disciples of the Lord.

God has great respect for women, and according to the Bible, spoke to some of them directly, or through an angel, or in a dream. It was because of these brave and faithful women that the Good News of Christ spread like wildfire.

What follows is a list of women who are mentioned in the New Testament. They were persecuted more than men because they were women, but little is said about this in the Bible. This was actually the very beginning of women's rights in the ancient world. Not much is known about the women who helped start the Church, but nine are mentioned below that were disciples of Christ.

Mary, the Mother of Jesus

Mary the mother of James and Joses (Joseph) was also the mother of Jesus: **Matthew 27:55-56 (WEB)**, *Many women were there watching from afar, who had followed Jesus from Galilee, serving him. Among them were Mary Magdalene, Mary the mother of James and Joses, and the mother of the sons of Zebedee.*

This Scripture verse doesn't tell us that this is Mary, the mother of Christ. There are so many women with the name Mary that it's sometimes confusing. We know that James and Jude wrote books for the New Testament, but it's not clear what Joses did. We do know he was one of Christ's brothers and was named after his father, Joseph (Joses).

Mary, the mother of Christ, was certainly a believer in her first-born being the Son of God. We can safely assume that Mary was a bold witness and disciple of Jesus.

We don't exactly know the circumstances

surrounding the death of Mary. One theory suggests she died in Jerusalem. Another suggests she moved to Ephesus, where she is said to have lived prior to her death. This makes the most sense because she was being taken care of by John, who moved to Ephesus to preach the Good News.

Stories say that Mary didn't live in the city of Ephesus itself because she didn't care for the city lifestyle. She resided in a small house on a hill, next to a road that came from Jerusalem. It was built for her by John. Being near the road it's possible that many travelers who were believers in Christ stopped to pay homage to her. The area had many fertile fields, and nearby were homes with families who were friends. The small settlement contained both Jewish and Christian settlers who lived in tents or huts. It is reported that Mary's house was the only one built of stone.

One ancient text states that on the day of her death Mary was lying in her bed at home. She was old and had lived a fulfilling life as the mother of Jesus, and raising other children. The Apostles had assembled there to display their great respect for Mary, as they knew her time was near. They held a service for her as Peter, who stood in front of the others, led the group in prayer. The mother of Jesus peacefully passed away. She was buried close to her home in Ephesus. No one knows the exact location of her grave.

Mary, the mother of Jesus, will live forever in our hearts and minds. She truly is a Saint. She was selected by God to bear His Son.

Joanna

We know that Joanna was the wife of Chuza, the house-steward of Herod the Tetrarch. He was very well off because he worked for the king. Some writers identify him as the nobleman in **John 4:46-49 (WEB)**, *Jesus came therefore again to Cana of Galilee, where he made the water into wine. There was a certain nobleman whose son was sick at Capernaum. When he heard that Jesus had come out of Judea into Galilee, he went to him, and begged him that he would come down and heal his son, for he was at the point of death. Jesus, therefore, said to him, "Unless you see signs and wonders, you will in no way believe."*

The nobleman said to him, "Sir, come down before my child dies."

Jesus said to him, "Go your way. Your son lives." The man believed the word that Jesus spoke to him, and he went his way.

Joanna, Mary Magdalene, and Susanna were among the women who had been healed directly by Jesus. Whether Joanna had been possessed or had a physical disability, we don't know. It is evident that she was in the upper class because of her husband's position. She was restored to normal health by Christ, as well as her son. In turn for the miracles, she gave her life to him. She became a disciple of Christ.

Luke 8:1-3 (WEB), *Soon afterward, he went about through cities and villages, preaching and bringing the good news of God's Kingdom. With him were the Twelve, and certain women who had been healed of evil* *spirits and infirmities: Mary who was called Magdalene, from whom seven demons had gone out; and Joanna, the wife of Chuza, Herod's steward; Susanna; and many others; who served them from their possessions.*

Joanna became a disciple and traveling companion. She was the tip-of-the-spear, going ahead before Christ and the Twelve, to arrange for their reception in various cities. She paid for many expenses of the disciples with her own money. This is how she showed support to Jesus and freely gave all she had for his welfare.

Joanna was at the tomb, with the other women, that Sunday morning and saw it was empty. They recalled what Jesus had said: **Luke 24:7-10 (WEB)**, *"The Son of Man must be delivered up into the hands of sinful men, and be crucified, and the third day rise again."*

They remembered his words, returned from the tomb, and told all these things to the eleven, and to all the rest. Now they were Mary Magdalene, Joanna, and Mary the mother of James. The other women with them told these things to the apostles.

After the resurrection, Joanna continued to be a witness for Christ and a supporter of the disciples. It isn't exactly known what happened to her or how she died. Her faith was unstoppable.

Mary of Bethany

Mary was from Bethany, as was her brother Lazarus, and sister Martha. These three siblings were friends and disciples of Jesus. They were people who Jesus loved. Since the three lived together we can assume they had no spouses. One cannot tell the story about Mary without Martha and Lazarus.

The Jesus and the disciples were entering the village of Bethany. A woman spotted them and invited them into her house. She knew who they were right away, as the news about Jesus and his disciples had spread to every little village and city.

Luke 10:38-42 (WEB), *As they went on their way, he entered into a certain village, and a certain woman named Martha received Him into her house. She had a sister called Mary, who also sat at Jesus' feet, and heard his word. But Martha was distracted with much serving, and she came up to him, and said, "Lord, don't you care that my sister left me to serve alone? Ask her therefore to help me."*

Jesus answered her, "Martha, Martha, you are anxious and troubled about many things, but one thing is needed. Mary has chosen the good part, which will not be taken away from her."

Sometime later, an urgent message came from Bethany to Jesus. Mary and Martha wanted Jesus to come right away because Lazarus was sick and near death. Jesus made a strange comment that the illness would not cause death, but it would be for God's glory. Christ stayed two more days where he was instead of leaving right away. During this time, it was reported that Lazarus had died. Jesus told the disciples he was asleep and he would wake him. They said if he is only sleeping then he will get better. Finally, Jesus clearly told them that Lazarus had died, but they were still going to see him.

John 11:16 (WEB), *Then Thomas said to the other disciples, "Let us also go, that we may die with him."*

Since the area of Bethany was full of their enemies, Thomas was being sarcastic.

John 11:17-36 (WEB), *So when Jesus came, he found that he had been in the tomb four days already. Now Bethany was near Jerusalem, about fifteen stadia away. Many of the Jews had joined the women around Martha and Mary, to console them concerning their brother. Then when Martha heard that Jesus was coming, she went and met him, but Mary stayed in the house. Therefore, Martha said to Jesus, "Lord, if you would have been here, my brother wouldn't have died. Even now I know that, whatever you ask of God, God will give you."*

Jesus said to her, "Your brother will rise again."

Martha said to Him, "I know that he will rise again in the resurrection at the last day."

Jesus said to her, "I am the resurrection and the life. He who believes in me will still live, even if he dies. Whoever lives and believes in me will never die. Do you believe this?"

She said to Him, "Yes, Lord. I have come to believe that you are the Christ, God's Son, He who comes into the world."

When she had said this, she went away, and called Mary, her sister, secretly, saying, "The Teacher is here, and is calling you."

When she heard this, she arose quickly and went to him. Now Jesus had not yet come into the village but was in the place where Martha met him. Then the Jews who were with her in the house, and were consoling her, when they saw Mary, that she rose up quickly and went out, followed her, saying, "She is going to the tomb to weep there." Therefore, when Mary came to where Jesus was, and saw him, she fell down at his feet, saying to him, "Lord, if you would have been here, my brother wouldn't have died."

When Jesus, therefore, saw her weeping, and the Jews weeping who came with her, He groaned in the spirit, and was troubled, and said, "Where have you laid him?"

They told him, "Lord, come and see."

Jesus wept.

The Jews, therefore, said, "See how much affection he had for him!"

John 11:41-45 (WEB), *So they took away the stone from the place where the dead man was lying. Jesus lifted up his eyes, and said, "Father, I thank you that you listened to me. I know that you always listen to me, but because of the multitude that stands around I said this, that they may believe that you sent me." When he had said this, he cried with a loud voice, "Lazarus, come out!"*

He who was dead came out, bound hand and foot with wrappings, and his face was wrapped around with a cloth.

Jesus said to them, "Free him, and let him go."

Therefore many of the Jews, who came to Mary and saw what Jesus did, believed in him.

Word of this miracle spread rapidly to the Jewish leaders, who started making plans to seize Jesus. Those who were not there did not believe. It had to be some kind of trick. The story continues as Jesus, sometime in the future, has supper with the man who had died and risen.

John 12:1-8 (WEB), *Then six days before the Passover, Jesus came to Bethany, where Lazarus was, who had been dead, whom he raised from the dead. So they made him a supper there. Martha served, but Lazarus was one of those who sat at the table with him. Mary, therefore, took a pound of ointment of pure nard, very precious, and anointed the feet of Jesus, and wiped his feet with her hair. The house was filled with the fragrance of the ointment.*

Then Judas Iscariot, Simon's son, one of His disciples, who would betray him, said, "Why wasn't this ointment sold for three hundred denarii, and given to the poor?" Now he said this, not because he cared for the poor, but because he was a thief, and having the money box, used to steal what was put into it. But Jesus said, "Leave her alone. She has kept this for the day of my burial. For you always have the poor with you, but you don't always have me."

It should be noted that nard is a type of aromatic oil derived from the Valerian plant family. Since ancient times the oil has been used as a perfume.

We can assume that Mary did what she could to help Jesus. We know she showed Christ great respect and was pleased to be his servant. There is nothing further written about her discipleship in the New Testament. We can only assume she continued to praise Christ until her ending here on earth. She had strong faith, as did her brother and sister.

It should be noted that if Jesus, through God, raised Lazarus from the dead after four days ... then surely God could resurrect Jesus to walk among His disciples again before he ascended.

Mary Magdalene

One of the most beloved women disciples was Mary Magdalene. What we know of her comes mostly from the New Testament. She is believed to have been of Jewish background, but her behavior was more like a Gentile.

Many people know the story of Jesus casting the seven demons out of Mary. It was a touching Biblical moment. Mary was thrashing around on the ground, and Jesus commanded the demons to leave her. That is when she started to follow Christ and his teachings. Mary Magdalene is distinguished from all others with the same name by using the name of her birthplace, Magdalene. Mary was a key person in the New

Testament. She was a strong believer and follower of Jesus Christ.

Luke 8:1-3 (WEB), *Soon afterward, he went about through cities and villages, preaching and bringing the good news of God's Kingdom. With him were the twelve, and certain women who had been healed of evil spirits and infirmities: Mary who was called Magdalene, from whom seven demons had gone out; ...*

The Gospels of Matthew, Mark, Luke, and John place Mary as a witness to the crucifixion, burial, and resurrection of Christ. Mary Magdalene was one of the most loyal followers and is said to have been the first to witness his resurrection.

John 20:11-18 (WEB), *But Mary was standing outside at the tomb weeping. So, as she wept, she stooped and looked into the tomb, and she saw two angels in white sitting, one at the head, and one at the feet, where the body of Jesus had lain. They told her, "Woman, why are you weeping?"*

She said to them, "Because they have taken away my Lord, and I don't know where they have laid him." When she had said this, she turned around and saw Jesus standing, and didn't know that it was Jesus.

Jesus said to her, "Woman, why are you weeping? Who are you looking for?"

She, supposing Him to be the gardener, said to him, "Sir, if you have carried him away, tell me where you have laid him, and I will take him away."

Jesus said to her, "Mary."

She turned and said to him, "Rabboni!" which is to say, "Teacher!"

Jesus said to her, "Don't hold me, for I haven't yet ascended to my Father; but go to my brothers, and tell them, 'I am ascending to my Father and your Father, to my God and your God.'"

Mary Magdalene came and told the disciples that she had seen the Lord, and that he had said these things to her.

Mary was truly blessed to be the first to see the resurrected Christ.

Mark 16:9-11 (WEB), *Now when he had risen early on the first day of the week, he appeared first to Mary Magdalene, from whom he had cast out seven demons. She went and told those who had been with him, as they mourned and wept. When they heard that he was alive, and had been seen by her, they disbelieved.*

She was the first to tell the Good News to the disciples. That said, however, the Gospels differ slightly on what exactly transpired on that first Easter Sunday, and who was there. However, if you look at all the Gospels, making note of what they say, the following women were present: Mary the mother of James, Salome, Joanna, Mary Magdalene, and Mary the mother of Jesus. Perhaps the stories are a little unclear because of the shock, fear, and joy of the event.

In any case, we can just imagine what happened that early Sunday morning. The women met together to proceed to the tomb to clean and make ready the body of Christ. Or they all agreed to meet at the tomb at daybreak. There would certainly have been more than one woman there because they all loved Jesus, and they would be there to support their fellow believers. Together they would prepare the body and offer their final prayers for Jesus.

They arrived at the tomb, but a large stone that sealed the tomb was in the way. Suddenly, there was an earthquake and an angel appeared who pushed the stone aside. The women were shocked at what they saw.

Matthew 28: 2-7 (WEB), *Behold, there was a great earthquake, for an angel of the Lord descended from the sky, and came and rolled away the stone from the door, and sat on it. His appearance was like lightning, and his clothing white as snow. For fear of him, the guards shook and became like dead men. The angel answered the women, "Don't be afraid, for I know that you seek Jesus, who has been crucified. He is not here, for he has risen, just like he said. Come, see the place where the Lord was lying. Go quickly and tell his disciples, 'He has risen from the dead, and behold, he goes before you into Galilee; there you will see him.' Behold, I have told you."*

What happened to Mary Magdalene after Jesus went to the Father? According to some historical records, she accompanied John to the city of Ephesus, in modern Turkey, which makes sense because she would have been with Mary the mother of Jesus. It's possible that Mary Magdalene may have helped John care for the mother of Christ.

It is said Mary Magdalene died in Ephesus and was buried there. Maybe she was laid to rest near the Mother of Christ. But there is no Biblical record of this. Others claim she traveled and preached as far north as southern France. Again, there is no record that this actually occurred. Today she is considered a saint by the Catholic, Orthodox, Anglican, and Lutheran churches.

Mary Magdalene was a disciple of Jesus who stood by him until the end. She was a woman of true faith who was blessed by the Lord.

Salome

The name Salome basically means "peace." She was the wife of Zebedee, the fisherman whose son's were James and John, the apostles. They lived in Capernaum an important little village indeed.

New Testament Scripture doesn't mention if she is Jewish, or anything about her background. All we know is that she was the wife of Zebedee, and we don't know much about him either. We do know that he didn't stop his sons from leaving their fishing jobs to follow Jesus. That point is a very important because it was a family business, and he surely needed his sons to help run it. Neither did Zebedee stop his wife from following the teachings of Jesus. It is assumed that Zebedee also shared his family's views and was a believer in Christ.

Matthew 4:18-22 (WEB), *Walking by the Sea of Galilee, he saw two brothers: Simon, who is called*

Peter, and Andrew, his brother, casting a net into the sea; for they were fishermen. He said to them, "Come after me, and I will make you fishers of men."

They immediately left their nets and followed Him. Going on from there, he saw two other brothers, James the son of Zebedee, and John his brother, in the boat with Zebedee their father, mending their nets. He called them. They immediately left the boat and their father, and followed him.

Salome followed Jesus in Galilee and aided him. She appears to have been one of his disciples from the beginning. She had no doubt that he was the real Messiah. Salome asked Jesus for a favor.

Matthew 20: 20-22 (WEB), *Then the mother of the sons of Zebedee came to him with her sons, kneeling and asking a certain thing of him. He said to her, "What do you want?"*

She said to him, "Command that these, my two sons, may sit, one on your right hand, and one on your left hand, in your Kingdom."

But Jesus answered, "You don't know what you are asking. Are you able to drink the cup that I am about to drink, and be baptized with the baptism that I am baptized with?"

They said to him, "We are able."

Salome remained a faithful disciple of Jesus her whole life. She was present at the crucifixion, watching that terrible act from a distance, even after her two sons had withdrawn. They withdrew because they couldn't watch Jesus their leader, teacher, and Son of God suffer. They were in disbelief that this could happen. Why, oh why, did God let his Son suffer? We know why now, but they did not fully understand that Jesus was saving everyone from their own sins.

Salome and the other women most likely stood a considerable distance away because of the crowd and the Roman soldiers. The sight of Jesus nailed to the cross upset them. Can you put yourself in their shoes? Standing there watching your loved one being slowly killed. It is something that's difficult to talk about, let alone watch. As he hung there in great pain, Jesus made a comment: **Luke 23:34 (WEB)**, *Jesus said, "Father, forgive them, for they don't know what they are doing."*

Salome was one of the women who came that Sunday morning at daybreak to anoint the body of Christ.

Mark 16:1-4 (WEB), *When the Sabbath was past, Mary Magdalene, and Mary the mother of James, and Salome, bought spices, that they might come and anoint him. Very early on the first day of the week, they came to the tomb when the sun had risen. They were saying among themselves, "Who will roll away the stone from the door of the tomb for us?" For it was very big. Looking up, they saw that the stone was rolled back.*

Entering into the tomb, they saw a young man sitting on the right side, dressed in a white robe, and they were amazed. He said to them, "Don't be amazed. You seek Jesus, the Nazarene, who has been crucified. He has risen. He is not here. Behold, the place where they laid him! But go, tell his disciples and Peter, 'He goes before you into Galilee. There you will see him, as he said to you.'"

After seeing the angel and finding out that Christ had risen, they hurried to tell the Good News to the disciples. It was a miracle and most likely their hearts were filled with joy.

Salome's son John wrote five of the books in the New Testament. John was also the caretaker of Mary, the Mother of Jesus. His book Revelation is the last book in the Bible. Here John is writing about what he has witnessed, which was a vision from Christ while he is on the island of Patmos.

Revelation 1:17-18 (WEB), *When I saw him, I fell at his feet like a dead man. He laid his right hand on me, saying, "Don't be afraid. I am the first and the last, and the Living one. I was dead, and behold, I am alive forevermore. Amen. I have the keys of Death and of Hades.*

It is clear that Salome and her husband were loyal and faithful followers of Christ. Being a good mother, she helped her sons, James and John, to become apostles of Jesus. This was a family united in one cause, which was to tell everyone about the New Covenant and their Savior Jesus Christ.

Susanna

The name Susanna means "white lily." Her name is actually only mentioned one time in the New Testament, in the Gospel of Luke.

Luke 8: 1-3 (WEB), *Soon afterward, he went about through cities and villages, preaching and bringing the Good News of God's Kingdom. With him were the Twelve and certain women who had been healed of evil spirits and infirmities: Mary who was called Magdalene, from whom seven demons had gone out; and Joanna, the wife of Chuza, Herod's steward; Susanna; and many others; who served them from their possessions.*

Susanna was one of the women Christ healed both physically and spiritually. She showed her gratitude by following Jesus and ministering to him along with his disciples. Although there is no proof, we can assume she wasn't married and had no children.

Ancient writings only tell us that Susanna was a virtuous and pure woman. Her parents were righteous and had strong Jewish faith. They taught their daughter the ancient Laws of Moses. A Jewish mother would carefully teach their children the ancient Scriptures and instruct them in practice of Jewish laws.

The disciples had all gathered together to select who would replace Judas. **Acts 1:14 (WEB)**, *All these with one accord continued steadfastly in prayer and supplication, along with the women, and Mary the mother of Jesus, and with his brothers.*

We can assume that Susanna was in attendance with all the other disciples at this important event. This showed how respected and important she was to the disciples. We know that all the women mentioned in the four Gospels are the same ones. They are the women who stood by the Lord at the cross and the ones who went to the tomb that early Sunday morning.

Susanna was one of these women. She was faithful until the end and after. She was indeed present and praying at the time of the Pentecost as she received the Holy Spirit.

Priscilla

Priscilla cannot be mentioned without bringing her husband, Aquila, into the story. Priscilla means "old-fashioned" according to research. This name has also been used as a family name in Roman history.

Note that Aquila, Priscilla's husband, had the family name of a Roman legion commander. His name means "eagle." This was the emblem used by the Roman army. So, both names were of Roman origin.

From Paul's second Epistle, written to Timothy, they are mentioned in **2 Timothy 4:19 (WEB)**, *Greet Priscilla and Aquila, and the house of Onesiphorus.*

What was the house of Onesiphorus? This refers to a man, and/or his family, by the name Onesiphorus. He was a very close personal friend of Paul's and helped him greatly. Onesiphorus means "bringing profit." His name is only mentioned twice in the Bible, both times in **2 Timothy**.

Early in the Epistle, Paul writes a prayer blessing Onesiphorus: **2 Timothy 1:16-18 (WEB)**, *May the Lord* *grant mercy to the house of Onesiphorus, for he often refreshed me, and was not ashamed of my chain, but when he was in Rome, he sought me diligently, and found me (the Lord grant to him to find the Lord's mercy in that day); and in how many things he served at Ephesus, you know very well.*

' From these passages, we know Onesiphorus was from Ephesus, where Paul had founded a church, and he helped Paul in many ways. His entire family must have been believers since Paul used the word "house."

Priscilla's background or history isn't mentioned in the New Testament. We do know her husband was born in Pontus, and most likely she was also. Both were Jews and were expelled from Rome by a ruling of Claudius. Rome was being cleansed of all Jews. It was in the city of Corinth that Priscilla and Aquila first became acquainted with Paul.

Paul discovered them when he came to Corinth from Athens, where they had been driven out by an edict from Claudius against the Jews.

Acts 18:1-4 (WEB), *After these things Paul departed from Athens and came to Corinth. He found a certain Jew named Aquila, a man of Pontus by race, who had recently come from Italy, with his wife Priscilla, because Claudius had commanded all the Jews to depart from Rome. He came to them, and because he practiced the same trade, he lived with them and worked for that trade, they were tentmakers. He reasoned in the synagogue every Sabbath and persuaded Jews and Greeks.*

Priscilla and her husband were partners in faith, not only to preach the Words of Christ but also in their everyday life. There was a need at the time for lay workers like Aquila and Priscilla who were ready to be a witness for Christ.

Exactly when Aquila and Priscilla came to the Lord isn't known. Paul lived in their home for eighteen months. Certainly, they came to Christ during that time period with Paul's constant teaching of the Word of Christ. With Paul as their guest, they must have prayed together and discussed Jesus at great lengths. The last mention of Priscilla and Aquila in the New Testament is also in **2 Timothy 4:19**, when they returned to Ephesus, around AD 66.

Ancient information advises us that they did lay down their lives for Christ, and were beheaded outside of Ephesus. No other details about their deaths could be found. What faith and love they had in Christ and for Paul, their friend, and brother in Christ. They were blessed by the Lord with eternal life.

Junia

There has been much debate over whether Junia was a woman or a man. This question arose because some of the Scriptures had added an "s" to the name, making it Junias, which makes it masculine.

No one knows why this was done. It is known that the masculine form of the name Junia was non-existent during ancient times. The feminine form was commonly used. Recently, Biblical scholars have agreed that the name is definitively feminine. However, the debate still lingers on for some reason.

At the end of **Romans**, Paul mentions many people he knows who were all involved in the ministry of Christ. They were either in Rome or from the Roman Empire. One of these people is Junia.

The only reference in the New Testament made of Junia is in **Romans 16:7 (WEB)**, *Greet Andronicus and Junia, my relatives and my fellow prisoners, who are notable among the apostles, who were also in Christ before me.*

Does Paul call them his relatives because he loves them so much, or are they really related? We don't know. Junia was taken prisoner for her beliefs, as was Andronicus and Paul. Junia's ministry with Andronicus and Paul, was indeed a close one. She was an equal with the men in their eyes and the eyes of the Lord.

Many Biblical scholars believe Andronicus was her husband, although there is no mention of that in any of the texts. He may have been a relative or close friend.

Read the following carefully again, as it states that Junia became a Christian before Paul did: **Romans 16:7 (WEB)**, *Greet Andronicus and Junia, my relatives and my fellow prisoners, who are notable among the apostles, **who were also in Christ before me.***

Paul came to believe some years after Christ had risen to the Father. Junia must have been one of the early converts to Christianity. More than likely she was one of the founders of the church in Rome.

Junia may have traveled to Jerusalem for the Passover and saw the crucifixion of Christ. Possibly, she was converted in Jerusalem at that time. It is known that the Roman Church was established before Peter and Paul traveled there.

The **Book of Romans** is a letter to the believers in Rome stating that Paul will come to visit soon.

Romans 1:7-10 (WEB), T*o all who are in Rome, beloved of God, called to be saints: Grace to you and peace from God our Father and the Lord Jesus Christ.*

First, I thank my God through Jesus Christ for all of you, that your faith is proclaimed throughout the whole world. For God is my witness, whom I serve in my spirit in the Good News of His Son, how unceasingly I make mention of you always in my prayers, requesting, if by any means now, at last, I may be prospered by the will of God to come to you.

At the time the church in Rome it was underground because it was illegal to be a Christian. However, many were meeting in secret and Paul wanted to go there to demonstrate support for their faith. It is possible that Junia was one of the first Christians in Rome.

Paul continues advising his longing to visit Rome: **Romans 1:11-12**, *For I long to see you, that I may impart to you some spiritual gift, to the end that you may be established; that is, that I with you may be encouraged in you, each of us by the other's faith, both yours and mine.*

We can conclude that Junia was an apostle before Paul and a strong believer in Jesus the Christ. It is possible that Junia was one of the disciples and/or a witness to the resurrection. Paul states that Junia was *"outstanding among the apostles."* It would be great to know more about Junia, Andronicus, and the founding people of the church in Rome, but there are few records on this subject. Nero destroyed most of the records related to Christianity, blaming them for the burning of Rome.

Many believers in the times of Christ accepted and honored women ministers of God. Junia was such an outstanding apostle that the Roman and/or Jewish persecutors imprisoned her to stop her from preaching the Good News. She and Andronicus were released from prison but continued to teach about Christ.

It is unfortunate, but there is no concrete information as to how or where they died. But they are alive with Christ and their names will live on in the Bible forever.

Phoebe

The name Phoebe means "pure" *or* "radiant like the moon." Little is known about her other than she was a student of Paul's, a deacon, and a devout Christian. She delivered Paul's letter to the Christians located in Rome. This was a trip that was long and somewhat dangerous for a woman at the time.

Paul provided her with a fantastic letter of

introduction to the Church of Rome.

Romans 16:1-2 (WEB), *I commend to you Phoebe, our sister, who is a servant of the assembly that is at Cenchreae, that you receive her in the Lord, in a way worthy of the saints, and that you assist her in whatever matter she may need from you, for she herself also has been a helper of many, and of my own self.*

Paul stressed, *"You assist her in whatever matter she may need from you."* Phoebe was Paul's sister in faith, so he wanted the church to accept her as an equal.

Exactly when Phoebe became a Christian and servant of the Lord is a mystery. "Our sister" is a term indicating she is a Christian. Some texts state that she had the designation as a deacon. That was a respected high position within the church. Whether or not Phoebe actually held the title of deacon isn't known. It is known that she was a trusted member of the church in Cenchreae, which was a seaport city a short distance from Corinth.

The New Testament hints there are two official positions within the church. One is a pastor or bishop, and the other is a deacon. The deacon's role is that of a servant to the church or even a lay minister. The title bishop generally means "overseer" and pastor means "shepherd." Therefore, a deacon is one who serves the church. A deacon must have excellent moral character, strong faith, and be trustworthy. They must set a good example in the community. Deacons are usually well-respected members of the church.

Paul's letter says that Phoebe helped many. We can

assume that she aided the sick, widows, orphans, and the poor who were important in the eyes of the Lord. Phoebe most likely was a great assistance to Paul in his duties.

Whatever her exact role was in the church, her name will live forever in **Romans 16** as a testimony to her life given to serve Christ. Now two thousand years later, we are still discussing the name of Phoebe. She will never be forgotten.

CHAPTER 9

MODERN-DAY TRUE STORIES

The following true stories were provided by the people who witnessed these events first hand. They have been rewritten by the author in the first person, taking care to be as accurate as possible.

A Memorial Day Story (A Holy Spirit)

Over a year ago my wife and I attended the local annual Memorial Day service, like we always do, honoring our military people who have served and died for our country. We went to Bay Pines National Cemetery in St. Petersburg, Florida, which always has a large crowd attending the service. Each year two or three thousand people visit to pay respects to the men and women who served our country.

It was a bright sunny day, not a cloud in the sky, as the service started. There are times when you can feel God is near you. This was one of those times. Everyone said the Pledge of Allegiance, sang the National Anthem and prayed together. It sent chills down my spine, and my whole body felt electrified, giving me goose-bumps.

I usually get that feeling when I am attending church or some holy event. Sometimes just listening to spiritual music brings on that feeling. I believe it's the Holy Spirit running through my body.

The service normally lasts about two hours and includes a local high school band supplying the military music. Speeches are given by many people, with the keynote address being provided by a military general.

My wife and I were sitting on the grass under a big oak tree in the shade. The shade provided relief from the sun. Most people were actually sitting in the hot sun, on the chairs that were set-up. We were off to one side and standing near us, under the tree, was a young man with his wife and little daughter.

I could tell he was in the military by his hair-cut and by the way he saluted the flag while standing at attention. Their little girl was playing and running around the tree, not paying much attention to the proceedings. However, she saluted the flag just like her dad did and said the Pledge of Allegiance. His daughter watched his every move. It was clear she wanted to be like her father. They seemed like a nice, typical American family. I smiled at him and he returned the smile. Even though I didn't know him, we had a bond that could be felt.

My wife watched their little girl, who came over and said hello. She touched my wife's arm and they talked for a little bit. I thought, what a sweet little girl. Her mom and dad told her not to bother the nice lady. So, she skipped around the tree softly singing a tune that

I didn't know.

The service ended, leaving all with a wonderful feeling that we were proud to be Americans and were very thankful for those that gave everything. People slowly made their way to the parking lot. We walked on the sidewalk next to the cemetery grass, where the flat grave markers laid close by, within thirty feet of us. The young family was walking just in front of us as the mass of people slowly moved along.

The little, brown-haired girl walked hand-in-hand with her dad. Being right behind them, I noted she suddenly let go of her father's hand. He didn't notice what she did next, but I did. She quickly proceeded to the grass and walked toward one of the grave markers. Her dad finally stopped walking when he saw her move onto the grass. He told her to come back.

She replied, "Just a minute, Daddy," as she kept walking.

Since they had stopped walking, we stopped too. We watched her, wondering what she was doing. She kept walking further out onto the lawn, not looking at her parents. She seemed focused on one grave marker.

Her mother said, "Come back here, right now. Don't walk on the grass."

"Okay, just a minute, Mommy." She continued on towards one of the gravestones. She made a bee-line to one about forty feet away.

Her father looked at me, and I at him. He shrugged his shoulders and patiently stood there waiting for his daughter. I smiled and shrugged my shoulders. I felt like I knew him since we had been together for a few hours.

We stood next to them and watched as their small daughter reached the gravestone and then stood on top of it. She was looking straight in front of her at something, but there was nothing there.

Then she started to giggle and speak. She was clearly talking to someone we couldn't see. She reached out with her hand, as if touching something. I could see her lips moving and hear her voice, but I couldn't make out the words. Her voice was very soft, all most a whisper.

Her mother told her, "Come here, right now!"

"Mommy, when I finish talking to this man," she said.

I noted that her father held his wife's arm to keep her from going to fetch their daughter. We stood there watching in wonder. By now several other people were taking notice of the event. I stared at the child and looked at her surroundings. The sun was shining and there wasn't a breeze in the air. At the time, it didn't occur to me what was exactly happening. I thought she was just playing, like kids do.

After a few minutes I clearly heard the girl say, "Thank you, goodbye now," and she skipped back across the grass to her parents with a smile on her face.

I overheard her mother ask, "Who were you talking to?"

She pointed back at the grave and replied, "That nice man, Mommy."

Everyone looked back at the grave. A sudden soft breeze blew up. The parents didn't say a word. Her father scooped her up into his arms and hugged her. Then they quickly walked away. I sensed he knew what had just transpired.

My wife and I stood there wondering, what had just happened? Clearly, she was talking to someone. Some holy spirit that we couldn't see, but she could. She saw something there on that grave marker. Was it a ghost? Was it Jesus? Was it an angel? Was it the spirit of a soldier? Was it God Himself? What did he say to her? Why did he call her over? I often think about those questions.

I turned around and searched the crowd for the family, but they were gone. They had simply blended into the mass of people and disappeared. As we walked away I was thinking about the incident. Did it really happen, or was she just a little girl playing?

I came to realize that of course an angel or spirit would speak to a little girl. Who better than a child, who is pure of heart, would be able to see and speak to a Holy Spirit?

I plan to return someday to find out which grave marker that was. Whose name is on that marker? But, in a way, it doesn't matter, because I know God was there, or one of his angels. As I said earlier, I could feel his spirit electrifying my body on that Memorial Day.

Angels Are Real (An Angel in Human Form)

At one time I wasn't a very religious man. However, I do believe in God and Jesus Christ. I do believe in miracles and praying. As far as angels go I always thought they were just in heaven. I have never seen one, but read about them in the Bible. I never gave much thought to angels being here on earth.

My mother knew the Bible inside out, and I got my beliefs from her taking me to Sunday school each week. She was diagnosed with Alzheimer's over ten years ago. I didn't believe it at first, but she had a slight form of it. I watched her degrade over the years until she had to go into a nursing home. I knew a little bit about nursing homes as both of my grandmothers passed away in nursing homes. My father and mother would go visit them almost every day to make sure they were being well treated. They would take them small gifts for birthdays and holidays.

Now it was my turn to do the same for my mother. My father passed away in 1988, so my mother only had her two sons to help her. I would be there for my mother no matter what. I moved from out of state to be close by and do whatever I could to help her.

One day she was found by the police walking the streets near her home at 2 am. The police asked her where she was going. Mom advised them to Chicago. That was her hometown, where she was born. I decided that was the final straw; she needed full-time care. As much as I hated to put her in a home, I had no choice at the time.

I was worried about the care she would receive. If you haven't been in a nursing home, I can assure you it is not a happy place, and in some cases, it's a depressing place to be. Most nursing homes smell like urine or bleach. People with memory problems wear special bracelets that activate and lock the doors, so they can't walk out. Some of the residents are still active and walk around a little, but most do not speak or interact to any great degree.

I also wondered about the people working there. Do they really care about the old people? The helpless, tired, old people who have nothing to live for, not even their memories. Most of these people can't even remember where they are and in many cases who their family is. That is scary to me. Imagine how they feel being scared every day, not knowing what is going to happen to them. Strangers are waking them up, feeding them, changing their clothes, and changing their diapers. Do they know deep inside their old brains, what is going on? Are they terrified every day?

How do those nurses and attendants deal with this depressing situation? The nursing-home workers are very important to provide these elderly people a decent quality of life in the time they have left. Screening of these people for employment is very necessary. I have heard some very distressing stories how some elderly are mistreated.

To make sure my mother was treated well, I would visit her four times a week. I did this for five years. As time went by I came to know the nursing staff taking care of my mother and the other people in her section. I was very pleased that the staff seemed loyal to their work and took excellent care of everyone. From time to time, one of the elderly would pass away and you could feel the sense of loss by the staff.

Once every week or two, I would take cakes, pies, or some chocolate for all to enjoy and give the nursing staff a little extra. I made it a point to talk to everyone, and somehow, I would pop out jokes to counter the depressing atmosphere. Sometimes I would read a book out loud or tell a story. Other times I would sing a song, and I could see some of their faces light up.

My mother fell in the middle of the night going to the bathroom and broke her upper leg and arm. It wasn't a good sign, and I thought she would die from the operation in the hospital. The doctor said she might not walk again after being in bed for three months. He was right and this was the beginning of the end for Mother. I saw the same thing happen to my grandmother. When you can't walk and get around you have pain all the time, and basically have no reason to live. You are bedridden which means many other health complications will develop. She was doomed, and I couldn't help her. As much as the therapists and I tried to get her to walk, she didn't have the strength, or the will, to lift herself up in bed.

About a month later mother was going downhill fast, not eating, and drinking very little. The head nurse, Andrea, who was newly assigned to this section, told me she could pass any day. Andrea kept close watch over my mother. There was something about Andrea that I liked. She was kind, spiritual, and always happy, showing a big smile all the time. She was sure my mother would go to heaven. She advised me not to worry because Mother would be in a better place and wouldn't suffer any-more.

I received a call at 2 am informing me that Mother had passed. It was from Andrea. This was strange because she worked days. Andrea told me she had worked that night because she knew Mother would pass, and wanted to be there to say some prayers and hold her hand. She wanted to open the window to let Mother's soul go out to heaven. Some people believe that is necessary.

At the celebration of Mother's life, in a small chapel, there were about sixty people in attendance. As I spoke about my mother, her life, and accomplishments, with tears in my eyes, I looked out in the crowd of seated mourners, and my eyes locked onto an almost glowing body smiling at me.

It was Andrea, which surprised me because I didn't expect to see her. Peace came over me. Totally unplanned I found myself telling everyone that in my mother's last moments she was with an angel who held her hand and helped guide her to heaven.

Yes, I do believe in angels; some are right here on earth in human form. Was Andrea really an angel? I don't know for sure, but I would like to believe that God sent her.

Where is this angel now? I don't know for sure. But

I know wherever she is, someone is being blessed. She is helping other souls pass on to heaven. Yes, angels can take the form of a human, so the Bible tells us. You may have seen an angel and didn't even know it. God's helpers could be anywhere.

A Miracle (Prayers Cure the Impossible)

Do you pray? Do you believe in miracles? God works miracles in many ways, I am told. I believe in miracles, so let me tell you my story. It's not a story about me per se, but about my son.

In 1984 my son was one of the leading male gymnasts in the country. At fifteen he won the AAU Junior Olympic Championships, and in the USGF (United States Gymnastics Federation) competition placed fourth in the country. He was rated one of the top male gymnasts in the country. He was invited to the Olympic Training Center in Colorado Springs for advanced training during the summer that year.

He had a dream to go as far as he could in this career. Things were going well, and it looked promising that if he didn't make the Olympic Team, he'd at least obtain a college scholarship. He had no fear of the dangerous tricks he was doing. He loved flying through the air doing a double back and landing on his feet. But, I did have fear watching him train, since he was 7 years old. Gymnastics, I came to find out, takes a toll on the body and can be dangerous. He trained almost most every day, and I was concerned because children, some that we knew, were injured over the years.

One day, doing a simple backflip during practice, he landed on his neck. He got up but had a lot of pain in his upper neck. His coach said we should have a doctor look at him just to be safe, so he called the best orthopedic doctor for sports medicine in the area, just to have it checked out. This doctor, whose clients were pro football and baseball players, was one of the best around. We didn't think it was anything very serious, just a sprained neck.

The next day we went there and they took X-rays. In those days that was all they could do as there were no MRI's or modern technology like there is now. The coach, my son, and I sat there waiting for the X-ray results in the doctor's office. After about an hour the doctor came in and said, "I have bad news for you. Your boy will never play any type of sport again. He has permanently damaged the ligaments between the first and second vertebrae. I believe they are torn. Any sudden head motion could cause the upper spine to touch the spinal cord, and he could become a paraplegic."

The doctor had a nurse come in with a metal neck brace and told my son he must wear this brace, possibly forever, if he didn't want to become crippled. We were all stunned by the bluntness of the doctor's comments. All three of us started to cry. I hugged my son with tears running down my cheeks.

I ask the doctor, "Are you sure? Are you positive? It seems impossible that little fall could do so much damage."

The doctor advised he had two other orthopedic doctors on the staff confirm the results by reviewing the X-rays. There was no doubt about the problem. The only other way to confirm it would be to perform surgery and have a look-see, but the damage cannot be repaired. So why risk surgery, because it may make the problem worse.

We went home to tell the terrible news to his mother. I think she went into shock, becoming speechless as I told her the doctor advised our son to wear the brace at all times. He could only take it off when sleeping, while using a special pillow. Our son said his neck didn't hurt so much and he was fine. He was in denial. I told him we'll get another doctor's opinion, and if necessary we'll go to the best doctor in the world. My wife and I both felt guilty about getting him into gymnastics. It was a terrible feeling eating away at us.

That night I prayed, we all prayed, for this nightmare to go away. I prayed every day for some answer or something to make this a better situation. I never prayed so much in my life. I even prayed in the car every day, while driving one hour to work and back. This haunted me and we needed God's help. I made a pact, an agreement, with God that if He helped my son, I would never ask Him for anything else for myself. I only cared about my family.

I started calling every doctor in the phone book. Remember, we had no internet back then. I phoned all my friends asking if they knew a doctor who specialized in necks and backs. I found four new doctors, and we went to each one over the next three months. The answer was the same: keep your brace on as it will never get better. Three long months had passed by with no hope in sight. We now had seven different doctors' opinions, who were all in agreement.

Two months later, one day at work, I was talking to a friend of mine about what happened and he advised me that his little boy had scoliosis and went to a back specialist named Dr. Brown. I got his number and called his office. To my surprise, his secretary put him on the phone right away. I told him the whole story and Dr. Brown told me to bring in the X-rays, along with my son, the next day at 9 am sharp. Being able to see this doctor right away was very unusual as people usually had to wait for a month for an appointment.

Dr. Brown looked at the X-rays and then took my son to take more X-rays and do some testing. I sat there, in the waiting room, praying the whole time. I was worried because this was the last doctor on my list. There was no one else to help him.

Peace came over me in the waiting room. I accepted the fact that whatever the doctor told us, no matter what the outcome, God had a reason for it. I simply said, "We are in your hands, God. Please help my son. I beg you to heal my son's neck. I will never ask for anything else."

They came back into the office, and Dr. Brown looked at me and said, "I have good news. There's nothing wrong with his neck. He should take the brace off and start on a neck exercise program for a month before going back into gymnastics."

I said, "What are you talking about? Are you sure?"

Brown advised he was 100 percent sure. If he had even a one percent doubt, he wouldn't recommend taking off the neck brace. He put everything in writing, setting himself up for a big lawsuit if he was wrong. He also gave me the name and phone number of the leading specialist in the country, located in New York City. The doctor advised us to go there for another examination if we had any doubt.

Dr. Brown told me that his daughter was my son's age, and she was a gymnast, and this was why he took a special interest in this case. He showed us the X-rays he took and the ones taken before, and there was a clear difference. He told us maybe the original X-rays weren't taken correctly, but he doubted that.

I asked him, "How could this be possible? A total of seven doctors said he needs the brace."

He replied, "If you believe in God, then it's a miracle."

I nodded. "Yes, I believe in God. It is a miracle." I immediately started to thank God and Jesus.

Was it a miracle? You can decide for yourself. I know it was a miracle. Yes, my son did go back into gymnastics, despite my worry and objections. Now years later, he is a gymnastics coach at a major university. Miracles are real. You just need to have faith in God.

God Works Wonders in Mysterious Ways
(A Toothache Saved My Life)

To most people, my story won't seem like a serious problem, but to thousands, it's a matter of life and death. In my lifetime I have seen five friends die of this disease. It slowly takes your mind and then your health. It ruins your family life and damages everyone close to you. This disease will suck you dry of everything near and dear to you. It drains your financial resources.

But you don't care what happens because you're too drunk. You are a big- time alcoholic. You drink to solve your problems and to forget what's eating at you. It might be your job or marriage problems you can't solve by yourself. There could be any number of reasons why you're killing yourself and damaging your loved ones. Or you may simply like to drink. You may love the burn that a shot of whiskey gives as you shoot it down. You may enjoy the feeling of being buzzed and take it to the point where you pass out. Or you may just want to kill yourself.

Most alcoholics simply can't stop drinking. It's a habit developed over a period of many years. It starts as a stress relief activity and turns into a socializing habit. Finally, after years of drinking, you are spending four or five hours sitting in a bar getting hammered every day. You're also spending five hundred bucks or more a month on your habit.

Let me tell you my story. Let me tell you how Jesus saved me from certain death. Yes, I was an alcoholic. Note, that I used the word "was" even though the group think in AA is to use the words, "I am an alcoholic." For me, that doesn't work. In my mind, I'm not an alcoholic any-more. I prefer looking at it that way.

You need to know I am a Christian and as a young man was a very active member of my church. Somewhere along the path of life, I lost my way with Christ. I became too busy trying to make a living and having a job that put me on the road a lot didn't help matters. I still believed in God and Jesus deep inside but just didn't show it on the outside. I stopped attending church. I quit praying.

I would stop at the local bar after work almost every day at 4 pm to have just one or two drinks. Then I would go home to have dinner with my wife. I never was a big drinker and didn't like getting drunk, in my younger days. I'd only drink at a party and never kept any booze at home.

As I became older I started going to the local bar earlier and earlier in the day. I stayed longer and drank more. Slowly, over a period of ten to twelve years, I was becoming drunk every day. My wife was having a hard time because of me. My drinking took a toll on her as well. She begged me to stop drinking. But alcoholics don't really care about other people. My feelings were drowned out by the booze.

Why did I take up drinking? At first, it started as a social activity, and then I realized I could drink my troubles away. My problem was retirement. I feared having no job and no income because I always had a job and plenty of money. I started three different businesses in my life and was burned out from working so hard, at least that's what I told myself. Starting over again seemed impossible. I was depressed, and drinking made it worse. At first, I didn't realize that, because the booze covered it up.

After a while, I decided to stop drinking. I could see what it was doing to me and my marriage. I told myself that I wouldn't drink today. But by 3 pm I needed a shot of whiskey and a beer. So, I would go and have one. Just one drink, I told myself. However, it doesn't work that way. One turns into two and two into three and so on. I lost all willpower and self-control and my body craved the booze.

This battle went on for years. Finally, I prayed to God for His help. I needed help to stop. Yes, I thought about going to AA, like one of my friends had, but I didn't. Every day I would get drunk, go home, have an argument with my wife, and fall asleep on the couch. I wouldn't even eat dinner. The next day I would pray to God for help.

I know God wanted to help me, but I forgot one thing. God only helps those who do not turn away and have faith. Months later I fell in the garage in a drunken state. I damaged my arm and knee. I couldn't raise my arm for months above my head. You'd think that would have made me stop drinking. No, it didn't, and I drank even more because of the pain in my arm.

I kept praying for God's help, to no avail. Then, a month or so later, I developed a terrible toothache a few days before Thanksgiving. I went to the dentist, and he said I needed to see an endodontist and have a root canal done. He made me an appointment, but it was a week later. Because of the holiday, I couldn't get in any sooner. I was in terrible pain. It was the worse pain I ever had in my life.

I go to the dentist every three months and have not had any problems in twenty years. I was surprised when this problem popped up out of the clear blue.

To ease my agony, I started taking over-the-counter pain relievers and aspirin in big doses and increased my drinking. I found out if I got drunk enough I would pass-out and could thereby sleep without any pain for a few hours. I prayed that God would help me.

I made it to the endodontist office and had the root canal done. I thought, great, no more pain! By now, after heavy drinking for a week, I felt like crap. The next day when the Novocain wore off, the pain was worse. It was a lot more intense, so I called the endodontist and he advised the pain would subside in a day or two. So, I had some more drinks and pain pills.

Sure enough, two days later I woke up and the pain had subsided. It was such a relief. I went to the kitchen, made a cup of coffee, and took an aspirin for my hangover. I felt much better as I sat down at my desk and turned on my computer to check my email.

Then all of a sudden, I started to sweat profusely. I was sweating from my head and chest mostly, which I thought was strange. I pulled out a thermometer and my temperature was slightly above normal. Checking my blood pressure, I found it was far too high, and my heart rate was extremely fast at one hundred eighty beats per minute (bpm).

I called 911 and just before they arrived I saw a bright light. I was here, but I wasn't here. It is hard to explain exactly what happened. I saw a flash of **pure white light**, just for a split second. It was fast, like a blink of an eye, but my eyes were open. I was standing when the white light hit me. My knees went weak and I was dizzy, but I never fell to the ground. It was indeed a strange feeling. I was worried and simply said, "God, please help me." I thought this was the end, but I didn't die. I was still fully awake.

I was dazed and sat down to gain my senses back as the paramedics arrived. They pulled out their equipment and advised me my heart rate was now 220, as I sat there feeling somewhat foggy headed. Amazingly, after a few minutes, my rate suddenly dropped back to 75, which is normal for me. I felt like myself again and the sweating stopped. The paramedics were surprised at how quickly my heart rate returned to normal. However, they recommended that I still go to the hospital, which I did.

After running all kinds of tests for two days, including scoping the inside of my heart and stress-testing it, the doctors were baffled as to why my heart started racing. The doctors found nothing wrong. As a matter of fact, all the tests, including lung X-rays, showed I was in perfect health. My heart and veins were clean and far better than normal for someone my age.

The cardiologist believed my episode had been

brought on by the pain pills and alcohol, along with stress from the toothache, which was entirely gone now. He advised me alcohol is more dangerous than smoking. One or two drinks a day is okay, but more than that can affect your health.

I didn't tell the doctor about the white light. I knew it was God that helped me. I knew it was God that answered my prayers. He gave me a warning sign to straighten up. I thanked God for helping me. After getting out of the hospital I immediately found a church my wife and I could attend.

I have not had the urge to drink since that day. God blessed me and took that demon out of my body with a flash of white light. Was it the Holy Spirit? I believe it was. It was like a dream, one that you can't recall exactly what transpired. Of course, I can never prove it was the Holy Spirit, but I don't need to prove it to anyone. I only know that God helped me stop drinking and saved my life with a toothache and a flash of **white light**. How else can I explain it?

I have renewed my life in Christ and I feel great. My marriage is better than ever. God makes big and small miracles in strange and amazing ways. You have to open your heart to receive his miracles and have faith. Thank you, Jesus!

CHAPTER 10

POWERFUL BIBLE SCRIPTURES

Please read these selected Scriptures, and choose those that you may need to use. Reading the Scriptures is the same as talking to God. He can hear you and will help your situation. These Scriptures cover the following: **salvation, loneliness, sorrow, suffering, decisions, danger, fear, weariness, temptation, and conviction**. Read these daily to help increase your faith.

Note: The following Scriptures are taken from Public Domain Versions. These may be copied and used as the Word of God.

FOR SALVATION

John 14:6 (WEB), *Jesus said to him, "I am the way, the truth, and the life. No one comes to the Father, except through me."*

Acts 16:29-31 (WEB), *The jailer called for lights, rushed in, and fell down trembling before Paul and Silas. He brought them out, and asked, "Sirs, what must*

I do to be saved?"

Paul and Silas replied, "Believe in the Lord Jesus Christ, and you will be saved, you and your household."

Romans 10:8-9 (WEB), *"The word is near you, in your mouth, and in your heart"; that is, the word of faith, which we preach. If you will confess with your mouth that Jesus is Lord, and believe in your heart that God raised Him from the dead, you will be saved."*

FOR LONELINESS

Psalm 23 (KJV), *The LORD is my shepherd; I shall not want.*

He maketh me to lie down in green pastures: he leadeth me beside the still waters.

He restoreth my soul: he leadeth me in the paths of righteousness for his name's sake.

Yea, though I walk through the valley of the shadow of death, I will fear no evil: for thou art with me; thy rod and thy staff they comfort me.

Thou preparest a table before me in the presence of mine enemies: thou anointest my head with oil; my cup runneth over.

Surely goodness and mercy shall follow me all the days of my life: and I will dwell in the house of the LORD forever.

IN SORROW

2 Corinthians 1:3-5 (WEB), *Blessed be the God and Father of our Lord Jesus Christ, the Father of mercies and God of all comfort; who comforts us in all our affliction, that we may be able to comfort those who are in any affliction, through the comfort with which we ourselves are comforted by God. For as the sufferings of Christ abound to us, even so, our comfort also abounds through Christ.*

Romans 8:28 (WEB), *We know that all things work together for good for those who love God, to those who are called according to His purpose.*

FOR SUFFERING

2 Corinthians 12:10 (KJV), *Therefore I take pleasure in infirmities, in reproaches, in necessities, in persecutions, in distresses for Christ's sake: for when I am weak, then am I strong.*

FOR DECISIONS

James 1:5-6 (WEB), *But if any of you lacks wisdom, let him ask of God, who gives to all liberally and without reproach; and it will be given to him. But let him ask in faith, without any doubting, for he who doubts is like a wave of the sea, driven by the wind and tossed.*

Proverbs 3:5-6 (KJV), *Trust in the Lord with all thine heart; and lean not unto thine own understanding.*

In all thy ways acknowledge him, and he shall direct thy paths.

IN DANGER

Psalm 91:1-6 (KJV), *He that dwelleth in the secret place of the most High shall abide under the shadow of the Almighty.*

I will say of the Lord, he is my refuge and my fortress: my God; in him will I trust.

Surely he shall deliver thee from the snare of the fowler, and from the noisome pestilence.

He shall cover thee with his feathers, and under his wings shalt thou trust: his truth shall be thy shield and buckler.

Thou shalt not be afraid for the terror by night; nor for the arrow that flieth by day;

Nor for the pestilence that walketh in darkness; nor for the destruction that wasteth at noonday.

Psalm 121:1-2 (WEB), *I will lift up my eyes to the hills. Where does my help come from? My help comes from the Lord, who made heaven and earth.*

IN FEAR

Hebrews 13:5-6 (WEB), *So that with good courage we say, "The Lord is my helper. I will not fear. What can man do to me?"*

Isaiah 41:10 (WEB), *Don't you be afraid, for I am with you. Don't be dismayed, for I am your God. I will strengthen you. Yes, I will help you. Yes, I will uphold you with the right hand of my righteousness.*

Ephesians 6:10-12 (WEB), *Finally, be strong in the Lord, and in the strength of his might. Put on the whole armor of God, that you may be able to stand against the wiles of the devil. For our wrestling is not against flesh and blood, but against the principalities, against the powers, against the world's rulers of the darkness of this age, and against the spiritual forces of wickedness in the heavenly places.*

IN WEARINESS

Matthew 11:28-29 (WEB), *"Come to me, all you who labor and are heavily burdened, and I will give you rest. Take my yoke upon you, and learn from me, for I am gentle and humble in heart; and you will find rest for your souls."*

IN TEMPTATION

James 1:12-16 (WEB), *Blessed is the man who endures temptation, for when he has been approved, he will receive the crown of life, which the Lord promised to those who love him.*

Let no man say when he is tempted, "I am tempted by God," for God can't be tempted by evil, and he himself tempts no one. But each one is tempted when he is drawn away by his own lust, and enticed. Then the lust, when it has conceived, bears sin; and the sin, when it is full grown, produces death. Don't be deceived, my beloved brothers.

Galatians 5:19-21 (WEB), *Now the deeds of the flesh are obvious, which are: adultery, sexual immorality, uncleanness, lustfulness, idolatry, sorcery, hatred, strife, jealousies, outbursts of anger, rivalries, divisions, heresies, envy, murders, drunkenness, orgies, and things like these; of which I forewarn you, even as I also forewarned you, that those who practice such things will not inherit God's Kingdom.*

IN CONVICTION

1 John 1:7-9 (WEB), *But if we walk in the light, as he is in the light, we have fellowship with one another, and the blood of Jesus Christ, his Son, cleanses us from all sin. If we say that we have no sin, we deceive ourselves, and the truth is not in us. If we confess our sins, he is faithful and righteous to forgive us the sins, and to cleanse us from all unrighteousness.*

CHAPTER 11

IMPORTANT SUBJECTS WRITTEN IN THE BIBLE

Read and study these Holy Scriptures, which are God's Words. Learn what the Bible say's about: **Itself, God, Christ, Man, Heaven, Sin, Hell, Faith,** and **Life**. These scriptures may surprise you as everything about us can be found in the Bible. Read God's Words and talk to Him.

SCRIPTURE ABOUT THE BIBLE

2 Timothy 3:16-17 (KJV), *All scripture is given by inspiration of God, and is profitable for doctrine, for reproof, for correction, for instruction in righteousness:*

That the man of God may be perfect, thoroughly furnished unto all good works.

Psalm 19:7 (KJV), *The law of the Lord is perfect, converting the soul: the testimony of the Lord is sure, making wise the simple.*

SCRIPTURE ABOUT GOD

Psalm 99:9 (KJV), *Exalt the Lord our God, and worship at his holy hill; for the Lord our God is holy.*

1 Timothy 1:17 (WEB), *Now to the King eternal, immortal, invisible, to God who alone is wise, be honor and glory forever and ever. Amen.*

Isaiah 45:22 (WEB), *"Look to me, and be saved, all the ends of the earth; for I am God, and there is no other."*

Colossians 1:12-14 (KJV), *Giving thanks unto the Father, which hath made us meet to be partakers of the inheritance of the saints in light:*

Who hath delivered us from the power of darkness, and hath translated us into the kingdom of his dear Son:

In whom we have redemption through his blood, even the forgiveness of sins:

SCRIPTURE ABOUT CHRIST: HIS BIRTH, WORK, AND RESURRECTION

Matthew 1:21-23 (WEB), *She shall give birth to a son. You shall call his name Jesus, for it is he who shall save his people from their sins."*

Now all this has happened, that it might be fulfilled which was spoken by the Lord through the prophet, saying, "Behold, the virgin shall be with child, and shall give birth to a son. They shall call his name Immanuel"; which is, being interpreted, "God with us."

Luke 2:10-11 (WEB), *The angel said to them, "Don't be afraid, for behold, I bring you good news of great joy which will be to all the people. For there is born to you today, in David's city, a Savior, who is Christ the Lord."*

John 10:28-30 (KJV), "*And I give unto them eternal life; and they shall never perish, neither shall any man pluck them out of my hand.*

My Father, which gave them me, is greater than all; and no man is able to pluck them out of my Father's hand.

I and my Father are one."

John 14:6 (WEB), *Jesus said to him, "I am the way, the truth, and the life. No one comes to the Father, except through me."*

Luke 22:19-20 (WEB), *He took bread, and when he had given thanks, he broke it, and gave to them, saying, "This is my body which is given for you. Do this in memory of me." Likewise, he took the cup after supper, saying, "This cup is the new covenant in my blood, which is poured out for you."*

Luke 24:36-39 (WEB), *As they said these things, Jesus himself stood among them, and said to them, "Peace be to you."*

But they were terrified and filled with fear, and supposed that they had seen a spirit.

He said to them, "Why are you troubled? Why do doubts arise in your hearts? See my hands and my feet, that it is truly me. Touch me and see, for a spirit doesn't have flesh and bones, as you see that I have."

1 Corinthians 15:3-5 (KJV), *For I delivered unto you first of all that which I also received, how that Christ died for our sins according to the scriptures;*

And that he was buried, and that he rose again the third day according to the scriptures:

And that he was seen of Cephas, then of the twelve:

SCRIPTURE ABOUT MAN

Genesis 1:27 (WEB), *God created man in his own image. In God's image he created him; male and female he created them.*

Genesis 2:7 (WEB), *God formed man from the dust of the ground, and breathed into his nostrils the breath of life; and man became a living soul.*

SCRIPTURE ABOUT HEAVEN

Revelation 21:3-4 (KJV), *And I heard a great voice out of heaven saying, Behold, the tabernacle of God is with men, and he will dwell with them, and they shall be his people, and God himself shall be with them, and be their God.*

And God shall wipe away all tears from their eyes; and there shall be no more death, neither sorrow, nor crying, neither shall there be any more pain: for the former things are passed away.

Revelation 21:27 (WEB), *There will in no way enter into it anything profane, or one who causes an* *abomination or a lie, but only those who are written in the Lamb's book of life.*

SCRIPTURE ABOUT SIN

Romans 5:12 (WEB), *Therefore, as sin entered into the world through one man, and death through sin; and so death passed to all men because all sinned.*

Isaiah 59:2 (WEB), *But your iniquities have separated you and your God, and your sins have hidden his face from you so that he will not hear.*

Romans 3:23 (WEB), *"For all have sinned, and fall short of the glory of God"*

SCRIPTURE ABOUT HELL

2 Thessalonians 1:8-9 (KJV), *In flaming fire taking vengeance on them that know not God, and that obey not the gospel of our Lord Jesus Christ:*

Who shall be punished with everlasting destruction from the presence of the Lord, and from the glory of his power; ...

Revelation 20:15 (WEB), *If anyone was not found written in the book of life, he was cast into the lake of fire.*

SCRIPTURE ABOUT FAITH

Hebrews 1:6 (WEB), *When he again brings in the firstborn into the world he says, "Let all the angels of God worship him."*

Ephesians 2:8-9 (WEB), *For by grace you have been*

saved through faith, and that not of yourselves; it is the gift of God, not of works, that no one would boast.

Hebrews 11:1 (WEB), *Now faith is assurance of things hoped for, proof of things not seen.*

SCRIPTURE ABOUT LIFE

John 3:3 (KJV), *Jesus answered and said unto him, "Verily, verily, I say unto thee, except a man be born again, he cannot see the kingdom of God."*

John 3:36 (KJV), *"He that believeth on the Son hath everlasting life: and he that believeth not the Son shall not see life; but the wrath of God abideth on him."*

John 11:25-26 (WEB), *"I am the resurrection and the life. He who believes in me will still live, even if he dies. Whoever lives and believes in me will never die. Do you believe this?"*

John 3:16-18 (WEB), *For God so loved the world, that he gave his one and only Son, that whoever believes in him should not perish, but have eternal life.*

For God didn't send his Son into the world to judge the world, but that the world should be saved through him.

He who believes in him is not judged. He who doesn't believe has been judged already, because he has not believed in the name of the one and only Son of God.

CHAPTER 12

HOW SHOULD WE PRAY?

Sometimes you may wonder, Am I praying correctly? The Bible teaches us how to pray. Read the following from the Gospel of Matthew. God knows what you want before you pray.

Praying is more than just saying words. When praying, humble yourself to God and beg for forgiveness. Remember to thank God for the many blessings you have received from Him.

When ending your prayer, thank God for sending His Son Jesus Christ to save us. Many prayers end with, *"I ask this in the name of our Lord and Savior Jesus Christ, Amen."*

Matthew 6:5-13 (KJV), *And when thou prayest, thou shalt not be as the hypocrites are: for they love to pray standing in the synagogues and in the corners of the streets, that they may be seen of men. Verily I say unto you, they have their reward.*

But thou, when thou prayest, enter into thy closet, and when thou hast shut thy door, pray to thy Father which is in secret; and thy Father which seeth in secret shall reward thee openly.

But when ye pray, use not vain repetitions, as the heathen do: for they think that they shall be heard for their much speaking.

Be not ye therefore like unto them: for your Father knoweth what things ye have need of, before ye ask him.

After this manner therefore pray ye: "Our Father which art in heaven, Hallowed be thy name.

Thy kingdom come, Thy will be done on earth, as it is in heaven.

Give us this day our daily bread.

And forgive us our debts, as we forgive our debtors.

And lead us not into temptation, but deliver us from evil: For thine is the kingdom, and the power, and the glory, forever." Amen.

Matthew 21:22 (WEB), *All things, whatever you ask in prayer, believing, you will receive.*

Jesus and Matthew tell us exactly how to pray. If you have faith your prayers will be answered.

CHAPTER 13

UNLOCK THE DOOR OF FAITH ... GOD WANTS TO HELP YOU

If you have read this book then you have the basic keys to unlock God's power in your life. Throughout the Bible, the main point mentioned time after time and Scripture after Scripture is the need to have faith. One must believe in Christ, for without faith he cannot help you.

If you have faith in the Lord and really believe, then you will obey God's laws and rules. You will follow the teachings of Jesus and love one another. For with faith comes good deeds to help your fellow man.

What is real faith? Faith was discussed earlier in this book. But let us examine the Scriptures again to gain a better explanation.

About Faith

The following two Scriptures are describing faith.

Hebrews 11:1-3 (WEB), *Now faith is assurance of*

things hoped for, proof of things not seen. For by this, the elders obtained testimony. By faith, we understand that the universe has been framed by the word of God, so that what is seen has not been made out of things which are visible.

Hebrews 11:6 (WEB), *Without faith it is impossible to be well pleasing to him, for he who comes to God must believe that he exists, and that he is a rewarder of those who seek him.*

Faith Without Question

For examples let us start with Noah. God told him that He would destroy all the people for the sins being committed. Noah was told to build an Ark. Noah did not ask any questions about this to God. He just followed God's directions as stated in **Genesis 6:22 (WEB)**, *"Thus Noah did. He did all that God commanded him."*

Noah had faith without question. He built a large boat far from any water to carry his family and the animals of the earth as directed. So, God blessed him.

Abraham was tested by God to show his faith. He was ordered to take his son, Isaac, to the mountain and sacrifice him. God was directing him to kill his own son. Abraham followed God's command and did as the Lord said without question. At the last minute before he sacrificed his son an angel stopped him.

Genesis 22:10-12 (WEB), *Abraham stretched out his hand and took the knife to kill his son.*

Yahweh's angel called to him out of the sky, and said, "Abraham, Abraham!"

He said, "Here I am."

He said, "Don't lay your hand on the boy or do anything to him. For now, I know that you fear God since you have not withheld your son, your only son, from me."

This was faith without question. In ancient days burnt offerings were offered to God to repent for the sins one committed. Note that God cannot tolerate sin in any manner.

Since man is a sinful being, God decided to bring forth His Son to die for our sins, to help us come to the Lord for everlasting life. The only requirement to be forgiven for sin is that one must have faith.

Faith in Deeds

From **James 2:14-18 (WEB)**, *What good is it, my brothers, if a man says he has faith, but has no works? Can faith save him? And if a brother or sister is naked and in lack of daily food, and one of you tells them, "Go in peace, be warmed and filled"; and yet you didn't give them the things the body needs, what good is it? Even so, faith, if it has no works, is dead in itself. Yes, a man will say, "You have faith, and I have works." Show me your faith without works, and I by my works will show you my faith.*

Paul states in **Ephesians 2:8-9 (WEB)**, *for by*

grace you have been saved through faith, and that not of yourselves; it is the gift of God, not of works, that no one would boast.

We can conclude that with faith one needs to perform good deeds. We should not boast or brag about our good works.

Faith in the Son of God

From **1 John 5:1-5 (KJV)**, *Whoever believes that Jesus is the Christ has been born of God. Whoever loves the Father also loves the child who is born of him.*

By this we know that we love the children of God, when we love God and keep his commandments.

For this is the love of God, that we keep his commandments. His commandments are not grievous.

For whatever is born of God overcomes the world. This is the victory that has overcome the world: your faith.

Who is he who overcomes the world, but he who believes that Jesus is the Son of God?

Read these words from Paul written in **Romans 10:8-13 (WEB)**, *But what does it say? "The word is near you, in your mouth, and in your heart"; that is, the word of faith, which we preach: that if you will confess with your mouth that Jesus is Lord, and believe in your heart that God raised him from the dead, you will be saved. For with the heart, one believes unto righteousness; and with the mouth, confession is made* *unto salvation. For the Scripture says, "Whoever believes in him will not be disappointed."*

For there is no distinction between Jew and Gentile; for the same Lord is Lord of all, and is rich to all who call on him. For, "Whoever will call on the name of the Lord will be saved."

Comments

We know that faith is a blessing from God. We can accept his gift of faith or decline it. The choice is up to you. Obedience to God's commandments and faith are the two most important points. These two actions are the keys to unlock God's power.

However, there is much more you can do to show your faith and loyalty to Christ. The following activities are suggested: read God's Holy Words, pray every day, be thankful to God, be kind and generous to your fellow man, and follow the teachings of Jesus.

Reading the Scriptures daily is a key component that will help boost your faith. Reading the Scriptures is almost like praying. God can hear you reading His Words because it's like a direct phone call to Him. The more you learn about the Bible, the greater your appreciation for Jesus and God becomes. You are watering the tree of faith when you read the Bible, which will make it grow. Your faith will grow stronger and stronger as time goes on because you are feeding it with the Holy Scriptures.

Ending Prayer

Dear Heavenly Father,

Thank you for your many blessings. I pray that this book, which contains your Holy Words, meets with your approval. I pray that others will read this book and find faith, love, and understanding. May our thoughts and words be acceptable to you. I humbly ask this in the name of our Lord and Savior Jesus Christ. Amen.

A FINAL REQUEST

If you have enjoyed this book and found it interesting please email me at ThomasHWardbooks@gmail.com with your comments. If you have witnessed a miracle or seen an angel please tell me your story. Finally, I kindly ask you to provide a review of this book on Amazon Books. Thank you so much for reading *Unlocking God's Power*.

IN CLOSING

About two years ago, the idea of writing a book about the Bible suddenly came to me. I don't recall how or why the idea popped into my head. I tried to push it out of my mind. I thought, who am I to write about the Bible? The answer is simple: I am nobody. Two years later the thought was still with me. A voice in my head kept urging me on. It was becoming an obsession to write about the Bible and God's Words. The problem was I didn't exactly know what to write about. What could I say about the Bible? Then the title of this book *"UNLOCKING GOD'S POWER,"* came to me in a dream.

I began to formulate an outline of the book. It was clear to me that God was indirectly, but gently urging me on. I discussed this with several ministers and friends who said they thought it was a calling to be a witness for God and Christ. They encouraged me to write this book. They advised me that God was most likely using my communication and writing skills to spread his Word. Actually, I don't think my writing skills are anything special, but I am a thinker.

The Bible, the most amazing book ever written, can

be overwhelming for most of us. To comprehend the Word of God, one must study the Bible in detail, and that requires a lot of hard work and time. For most of us, this is almost impossible. That is why we have ministers and priests. These people of God devote a lifetime learning about the Bible. They attend theological seminaries for years to understand God's Word. These disciples of God help us to comprehend his laws and teachings. The main reason we attend church is to obtain clarity and explanations to the meanings of the Bible, so we can have a better relationship with the Lord.

Since many people don't attend church, it seemed logical to write a book that would make it easier for people to become interested in reading the Bible. I wanted to write a book that would spark people awake to the wonders of God and Jesus. I wanted it to be interesting and different, to make it a learning tool that people would enjoy.

People need to know the power of God's Words. People need to know that miracles are possible if you have faith and believe. Everyone should know the joy of accepting Jesus Christ as our Lord and Savior. God is waiting for you. He wants to help you have a better and more fulfilling life.

I wondered, why would God choose a sinner like me to do his bidding? Then I realized that maybe even God needs sinners, but loyal men with faith, to help spread his Word.

I pray this book meets with God's approval and receives His blessings.

ABOUT THE AUTHOR

Thomas H. Ward has been a passionate student of the Bible and of world history for fifty years. The author has published more than twenty books and forty articles. He is a layperson, former deacon, former church school teacher, and previously a Board of Director member for a United Church of Christ affiliate.

"Unlocking God's Power" is the first in Ward's **Biblical Series**. The next books planned are: *Mysteries of The Bible, Biblical Facts and Theories About the Lost Ark,* and *Evidence of the Resurrection.*

Ward is a best-selling author of fictional and non-fictional works. Nonfictional works include: *Real Life Adventures of Tommy and Ronnie* (a children's book), *Small Business Accounting Tools, Letters of Credit and Documentary Collections, The Race for Money* (a retirement investment guide), and *Gun Talk* (a thought-provoking book of common sense).

He is best known for his ten-book fictional series *The Tocabaga Chronicles* and *Templars Quest Trilogy* (a three-book series). Ward's newest books from his *"Asian Mystery Series"* are; *Critical Incidents* and *The*

Finger Collector, which was entered into an Amazon best fictional mystery story contest.

Education and Experience

Born in Chicago, he now resides in Tampa, Florida. Ward, prior to becoming an author, was a Metallurgical Engineer and business owner. He obtained an MBA in International Business.

Having traveled extensively to thirteen different countries, his favorite ones are China, Japan, and South Korea, where he was based for a period of time. He has made over one hundred fifty trips to Asian and Europe over a twenty-year time period, becoming conversant in three different languages. Thomas is an avid student of world history and the Bible.

Ward started writing technical manuals and business books years ago, then he turned to writing fictional stories when his publisher suggested he do so. "Thomas always had great stories to tell. His life experiences, travels, and imagination is a bonus for a fiction writer."

Ward always places in his books the following quote: *"In every truth there is non-truth and in every fiction there is non-fiction."*

BOOKLIST OF THOMAS H. WARD

*** NON-FICTION BOOKS***

GUN TALK: A THOUGHT PROVOKING BOOK OF COMMON SENSE

REAL LIFE ADVENTURES OF TOMMY AND RONNIE: A CHILDRENS BOOK

THE RACE FOR MONEY: INVEST FOR RETIREMENT

LETTERS OF CREDIT: HOW THEY WORK

SMALL BUSINESS ACCOUNTING TOOLS

AMERICAN GAIJIN: TRAVEL STORIES IN ASIA

FICTION BOOKS

THE FINGER COLLECTOR: Blood Money

CRITICAL INCIDENTS: The ROK Land of HAN

TEMPLARS QUEST 1: GHOST KILLER

TEMPLARS QUEST 2: THE ANCIENTS

TEMPLARS QUEST 3: LUCEM SANCTAM

TEMPLARS QUEST TRILOGY: THE LOST ARK (BOOKS 1-3)

TOCABAGA 1: THE COLLAPSE (REVISED EDITION)

TOCABAGA 2: THEOTERRORISM

TOCABAGA 3: WARM BLOOD – COLD STEEL

TOCABAGA 4: TALOS WARRIORS

TOCABAGA 5: THE QUISLINGS & ADROKTONES

TOCABAGA 6: THE DIMACHAERUS CLAN - MISSING IN ACTION

TOCABAGA 7: PÀN GUÓ ZUÌ - HIGH TREASON

TOCABAGA 8: THE INVISIBLES

TOCABAGA 9: THE CRIMSON CROSS

TOCABAGA 10: POWER OF THE SWORD

CONTACT

Thomas H. Ward, email:
ThomasHwardBooks@gmail.com

BIBLIOGRAPHY

INTERNET REFERENCES

http://truthbook.com/jesus/twelve-apostles/simon-the-zealot

https://www.biblegateway.com/resources/all-women-bible/Mary-Magdalene

https://www.openbible.info/topics/mary_of_bethany

http://truthbook.com/jesus/jesus-siblings-brothers-sisters

http://www.stjude-shrine.org/about

http://taylormarshall.com/2012/04/gruesome-death-of-saint-mark-evangelist.html

https://support.biblegateway.com/hc/en-us/articles/228180487-What-Bibles-on-Bible-Gateway-are-in-the-public-domain-

https://worldenglishbible.org/

https://www.reference.com/world-view/biographical-luke-bible-f5e20d7030f52376?qo=contentSimilarQuestions

http://biblehub.com/timeline/old.htm

http://d.lib.rochester.edu/camelot/text/history-of-that-holy-disciple-joseph-of-arimathea

https://www.biblegateway.com/versions/Douay-Rheims-1899-American-Edition-DRA-Bible/#vinfo

https://www.biblegateway.com/versions/American-Standard-Version-ASV-Bible/#copy

https://www.biblegateway.com/versions/King-James-Version-KJV-Bible/

https://www.biblegateway.com/versions/World-English-Bible-WEB/

https://www.biblegateway.com/versions/World-English-Bible-WEB/#copy

http://www.crosswalk.com/faith/bible-study/man-s-rules-vs-god-s-rules.html

http://www.biblestudytools.com/topical-verses/the-25-most-read-bible-verses/

http://www.whatchristianswanttoknow.com/famous-bible-verses-27-well-known-scriptures/

http://biblereasons.com/all-sins-being-equal/

https://www.openbible.info/topics/rules

http://www.bellshoalscoc.org/Elements-Of-Successful-Prayer

https://www.amazingfacts.org/media-library/storacle/e/5339/t/the-mark-of-cain

http://www.bibletimelines.net/article/145/available-timelines-sorted-by-category/moses-the-exodus-timeline

http://faculty.washington.edu/snoegel/PDFs/articles/noegel-ark-2015.pdf

https://simple.wikipedia.org/wiki/Ten_Commandments#Differences_in_teachings_and_interpretation

http://www.historyworld.net/wrldhis/PlainTextHistories.asp?historyid=aa11

https://www.biblicalarchaeology.org/daily/biblical-topics/bible-versions-and-translations/the-gospel-of-thomas-114-sayings-of-jesus/

http://www.shroud.com/

https://www.shroud.com/guscin.htm

https://bible.org/seriespage/6-zealots

https://oca.org/saints/lives/2016/06/19/101752-apostle-jude-the-brother-of-the-lord

BIBLIOGRAPHY

https://www.gotquestions.org/difference-disciple-apostle.html

http://www.christian-history.org/death-of-james.html

http://www.bibleinfo.com/en/questions/did-jesus-have-any-brothers-andor-sisters

https://www.gotquestions.org/Saul-Paul.html

http://www.biblearchaeology.org/post/2007/08/15/Three-Woes!.aspx#Article

http://www.bibleinfo.com/en/questions/who-were-twelve-disciples#matthew-levi

http://www.bibleplaces.com/capernaum/

https://www.whatchristianswanttoknow.com/what-happened-to-mary-the-mother-of-jesus-after-the-crucifixion/

http://www.mcv3.org/content/what-does-cenacle-mean

https://www.bibleplaces.com/bethsaida/

http://www.nationalreview.com/article/434153/shroud-turin-christs-blood-both-there-and-sudarium-oviedo

http://www.catholicherald.co.uk/issues/august-4th-2017/turin-shroud-the-latest-evidence-will-challenge-the-sceptics/

https://www.youtube.com/watch?v=yhFh5DPmJLo … **THE SHROUD**

https://www.youtube.com/watch?v=4LZRfUkw2VU … **THE SHROUD**

https://www.youtube.com/watch?v=diE9QjdEsN8 … **THE SHROUD**

http://www.newadvent.org/fathers/0805.htm

BOOK REFERENCES

The Complete Guide to the Bible, by Stephen M. Miller, Barbour Books Publishing, Inc.
The Gideon Holy Bible, known as the authorized *King James Version* (KJV)

The Holy Bible, known as the authorized *King James Version* (KJV)

The Holy Bible, known as *The New International Version* (NIV)

The Holy Bible, known as *The World English Bible* (WEB)

The Flight of the Holy Family to Egypt, by Fathy Saiid Georgy, introduced by Bishop Mettaos of the Saint Mary Syrian Monastery.

A.D. The Bible Continues, The Revolution That Changed the World, by Dr. David Jeremiah, Tyndale House Publishers, Inc.

A Story of God and All of US, by Roma Downey and Mark Burnett, Little, Brown, and Company Publishers.

www.ingramcontent.com/pod-product-compliance
Lightning Source LLC
Chambersburg PA
CBHW060919040426
42445CB00011B/702